Mama Said ♥♥♥♥♥♥ Because God Said It First

MAXIE FORTNER

CALVERT CITY, KENTUCKY

Bradley Scott Hall Publishing

Mama Said ♥♥♥♥♥♥*Because God Said It First*

Maxie Fortner

MAMA SAID ♥♥♥♥♥♥*BECAUSE* *GOD* *SAID IT FIRST*

Dedicated: To all ladies striving to teach Truth to the next generation

My hope ♥ is that this book will be used as a ladies' Bible class study guide and a personal memory record.

I pray it will be a springboard for:

♥A serious Bible study based on what God wants every generation to know

♥ A memory book to promote your own recording of memories important and trivial

♥ Lots of laughs and perhaps a tear if your memory warrants it

♥ Praise to God, Jesus and the Holy Spirit who gave us all we need for salvation and hope of eternity with them

♥ My family of origin and their descendants to smile in memory of Mama, Daddy, and other relatives, to laugh as we usually do when, "Do you remember" starts the conversation, and to pray with gratitude for the blessings we received.

PREFACE

The purpose of this set of lessons is to share with women of all ages the power of their own words and actions in the lives of our children, grandchildren and their peers. We *will* "pass it on." The message we present by our lives and our vocal expressions will resound through the years, even beyond our earthly lifespan. At best, our words will be a replay of the words of Christ living in us, and not just an echo growing dimmer with each generation.

At the time of this writing, four decades after her mortal death, my brothers, sister, and I continue to quote the expressions of our mother, to be referred to as Mama throughout this series of lessons. We have had the pleasure and security of faith that was shared with us from birth by her example and overt teaching. All six of her children became faithful Christians, have Christian mates, and all of us endeavored to pass that faith to the next generation, who are already extending the torch to the youngest generation, Mama's great-grandchildren. So far, all of Mama's grandchildren are Christians as well as the great-grandchildren who are of an accountable age. Some of the male descendants preach when the opportunity arises and all serve in one way or another. Please know that this is not being written with any sense of worldly pride, but with a monumental gratitude to God for His grace, for His continual forgiveness of our sinfulness through the sacrifice of His Son, and for the wonderful gift of Mama who lived each day with Him as a focus. This work could not have been written if she were alive; she was far too humble and would have been, in her words, "utterly embarrassed" by such public praise.

Mama was perfect, not because she was sinless, but because she prayed without ceasing for forgiveness throughout her life after becoming a Christian. She understood obedience, repentance, and forgiveness. The words of these lessons are important only as they repeat exactly the inspired word of God. I pray that we will make the Bible our guide, that the Word will be our blueprint for life, and that we will exhibit and extend our faith to generations following. Our paths will be followed by our most precious loved ones……May it lead to heaven.

Deut 4:9 Only be careful, and watch yourselves closely so that you do not forget the things your eyes have seen or let them slip from your heart as long as you live. Teach them to your children and to their children after them. NIV

ACKNOWLEDGEMENTS

"♪*I owe a debt I cannot pay*" to God, Jesus, and the Holy Spirit for salvation, to my mother, Sadie Louise Wilkerson Massey, who taught us truth, to Granddaddy, Rube Wilkerson, who taught her after he became a Christian as an adult, to my daddy, Ben Massey, whose favorite song, as well as mine, is *I Believe In the One They Call Jesus*. Perhaps I inherited my desire to write from Mama, who loved to write.

Until my nieces entered the picture, these lessons were written in basic form, but they gave me the motivation and courage to revise and publish. My thanks go to all seven of Mama's granddaughters: KaRen Coffman, Kelly Buchanan, Susan Pedersen, Dana Johnson, Sandy Faires, Kerrie Flowers, and Tracy Edmonson for writing their thoughts. A double thanks go to Sandy with her kind red pen and to Susan for her enthusiasm when I began...again...and again. Even my nephews unknowingly motivated this writing by their interest in the family stories I included in their Christmas cards.

My thanks go to my lifetime husband, Von, who urged me to write my first bit of public writing, a bit in our church bulletin. At age twenty I felt completely unqualified to write any sort of advice, hmmmm, I still do but I now realize the advice in the Bible is not my advice, or even Mama's.

My thanks go to my sons and daughters-in-law who encouraged the family stories and allow me to read to their precious children.

To my four brothers and sister, I love the life we spent together sharing Mama and Daddy, fun, work, relatives.....you get the picture. Thank you for laughing at the family memories! *It Won't Be Very Long* ♫ until we see our parents and Tommy again up there with Jesus.

Thanks to Kathy Cretsinger who gave me hope that this book really could be published and shared valuable information. How grateful I am to Brad Hall for his expertise and 'mind to work' in bringing this writing to publication. To Sandy Faires, who read and reread even during the publishing phase, I hope to return a small measure of this enormous favor.

1

MAMA SAID BE QUIET

Family Heartstrums ♥

Quiet times were rare. Brothers are noisy and so was I. Sometimes, Mama was, too. "Dick, Jack, Get up!" from downstairs. To the back of the house she would yell, "Max, Hurry up, I'll miss my ride!" To the garage with the basketball goal she might shout, "Tommy, Mark, supper's ready!" Farm life with no cell phones required a lot of 'hollering' to communicate without having to run back and forth.

Yet, Mama's communication philosophy which she often voiced in the car was, "If you can't say something good about someone, just don't say anything". When one is a part of a lively family or congregation or community made up of imperfect people, there is often some criticism and complaining floating around. We, siblings, often voiced our opinions to each other, rather loudly. "You always get to go!" "You're hogging all the seat!" "You always get the biggest piece!" "You're just a crybaby!" "Yeaaaa, two points!" "He's a tattletale!" "Bibbie and Earl Mack are here!" Not only did we tease and complain about each other, we often said unkind things about *individuals or laughed at some ridiculous thing that someone did at school. So you can see why Mama said, "Be quiet." We, kids, told each other to just shut up.*

Heart of the Matter ♥

Some gatherings fester gossip. One lady found it necessary to drop out of a carpool after one of the commuters privately questioned a troubled lady and then reported it with giggles. *Oh, to see ourselves as others see us (paraphrased from Robert Burns)*. Sometimes separating oneself from an ungodly situation is the most peaceful way out. How much better it would have been if the commuters had discussed a plan to brighten the day of their co-worker. In the same carpool, another lady often entertained the commuters with tales of her own inconsequential mistakes. Laughing at ourselves or making ourselves the butt of jokes brings empathy and laughter. Good news should spread as easily as gossip.

Remember something good that was said about you that affected your life. _____

_____

_____

Probably your favorite memory of Miriam is the scene in which she watches over her baby brother, Moses, and then approaches Pharaoh's daughter and offers to find a nurse for the baby. Or perhaps you love the scene where she sings to the women and leads them in a dance of joy and praise after Moses has led the Hebrew children between the two cliffs of Red Sea water on dry land. But the story doesn't end on that happy note.   Later in the wilderness, *Numbers 12,* Miriam shows she has a serious fault when she talks against Moses because he married a Cushite woman and she was struck with leprosy. Aren't we glad that Moses begged God to heal her! Before she was healed and brought into camp again God gave her a week of alone time to contemplate her behavior. That should make us think twice before criticizing one of our church leaders for something frivolous!

Old Testament Precedent

Please read these verses and jot down a key phrase you find relevant and discuss.

Prov. 10:18_____

Prov. 11:13_____

Prov. 16:28_____

Prov. 26:22_____

Prov. 18:8_____

Prov. 20:19_____

Prov. 26:20_____

In the Corinthian church, many sins prevailed that required Paul to write to them. To make a bad situation worse, gossip fueled the fire, destroying the unity that Christ prayed for the church to have. Gossip is a weapon used to intentionally harm, but is also injurious when careless words are spoken unintentionally. Moving out of a tongue-wagging situation may be difficult and may result in the loss of friendship, but we will be blessed by following God's word. Social occasions are more entertaining when conversations hold respect.

If an unpleasant situation must be reported, such as abuse cases, it is imperative that the person receiving the information be a person with the ability and authority to help the situation, not the general public. Professional people are trained to keep hurtful information confidential. As Christians, we must do likewise. *2 Cor. 12:20-21 For I am afraid that perhaps when I come I may find you to be not what I wish and may be found by you to be not what you wish; that perhaps there may be strife, jealousy, angry tempers, disputes, slanders, gossip, arrogance, disturbances; NASB*

Relate how gossip has harmed someone you know.

_____

_____

_____

_____

New Testament Admonition

Please read these verses and jot down a key phrase you find relevant and discuss.

Eph. 4:31_____

2 Cor. 12:20_____

Titus 3:2_____

Titus 2:3_____

Eph. 4:29_____

James 4:11_____

Romans 1:28-30_____

Have you ever walked into a room and noticed that the conversation came to a halt? It may be that gossip was interrupted or it may be that the participants knew that the one entering would not want to participate in an ungodly conversation. Teenagers are often victims of gossip and participants in the spread of gossip. Women have been labeled as being the most frequent gossipers, but men, unfortunately, are also guilty. Slander is spreading malicious information about someone with the intent to harm, but gossip, even when it is not intended to harm, does that very thing.

Words spoken can not be brought back and the thoughts and imaginations created inside the mind of the listener can not be turned off. Once I heard a young woman, in the midst of a negative conversation about other Christians, wisely suggest to the older women, "Let's stop and pray for them or else this is just gossip." One of life's embarrassing moments is when a son or daughter innocently repeats an unflattering opinion of someone to that very person.

Suggest a way we can answer when someone requests gossip from us.

Suggest a way we can tactfully stop someone who offers a tidbit of gossip to us.

Another facet of being quiet is remembering our place in God's plan for women. The women who were causing a ruckus in the church at Corinth were told to be quiet. A disturbance between factions of the body hinders the process of spreading the gospel and of spiritual growth in the congregation. If a church is in trouble and the women keep quiet then Godly men have a better chance to work through problems. Women sometimes speak with an emotional response without having pertinent information that the leaders have, thus causing more rifts and misunderstandings. Letting the men act in leadership roles without having women trying to run things makes the work easier.

1 Cor. 14:34-35 Let your women keep silent in the churches, for they are not permitted to speak; but they are to be submissive, as the law also says. 35 And if they want to learn something, let them ask their own husbands at home; for it is shameful for women to speak in church. NKJV

1 Tim 2:11 Let a woman learn in silence with all submission. 12 And I do not permit a woman to teach or to have authority over a man, but to be in silence. NKJV

When a man speaks with little insight on a subject, it may be difficult to keep quiet, but the scriptures admonish us to do our speaking at home, hopefully in a kind way, and allow the men to be leaders. If a woman insists on speaking her view publicly in the presence of men, she risks being in defiance of God. Even if a lady is more knowledgeable on a subject than the men in the assembly of God's family, not one is smarter than God.

One of God's greatest blessings is also a responsibility. It is our privilege as mothers and grandmothers to use our voice to teach our children, grandchildren and younger women. We teach each other daily as we interact with friends sharing ideas and experiences. Our voice is the means by which we confess our belief in Jesus Christ as the Son of God. It's with our voice that we express our love. It's our voice that praises God in song and prayer. It's our voice that compliments and brings happiness to others. It's our voice that soothes a distraught child or comforts the ill. It is also the woman's voice that should offer advice, even to men, when it is sought outside the assembly.

Share how someone used his or her voice in a way that made you laugh.

_____

_____

_____

_____

_____

The importance of supplying our children with good experiences and correct information from the Bible is immeasurable and the result is eternal. From our lips, our children will perceive what is in our hearts and from their lips we will know if their spiritual growth is taking place. If you want to know what is in your child's heart, then listen to what she says. Does she speak kindly or hatefully? Does he encourage or criticize? Does she praise or blame? Does he pray or curse? When you discover what comes from a child's mouth, then the next thing to discover is ***who set the pattern?***

Matt 12:34-35 For out of the abundance of the heart the mouth speaks. 35 A good man out of the good treasure of his heart brings forth good things, and an evil man out of the evil treasure brings forth evil things. NKJV

Report something good you have heard about someone in the room with you now.

_____

_____

Commitment: I, _____, will help

_____ use their voice in a way that brings

glory to God.

List five possible dangers we should teach children to report.

1. _____

2. _____

3. _____

4. _____

5. _____

Write It On Your Heart ♥ Memory verse: Ps 19:14 *Let the words of my mouth and the meditation of my heart. Be acceptable in Your sight, O LORD, my strength and my Redeemer. NKJV*

♥ **Mama's granddaughter, Susan Pedersen says**, "My favorite bumper sticker, WAG MORE, BARK LESS, sums it up. We need to listen to others and especially to God. The verse advising us to be silent and KNOW that I am God indicates that we should just hush, wait, and listen."

Take It To Heart ♥ Fictional Dilemma for Be Quiet

"...and then she said if I were smart I would know my multiplication tables by now. And I said I was just as smart as her and she didn't know everything because she missed 'spaghetti' on the spelling test and I got it right and I said I wouldn't play with her at recess and she said nobody liked me anyway and everybody would play with her and I cried. I don't want to go school another day. Sherry ruins everything!" So that was what the thunder cloud was all about. When Marianne came in from the bus, her face broadcast her heart. A bad day....a very bad day.

"Oh yes, just like her mother!" I thought, "The hedge apple doesn't fall far from the tree" and old hurts sprang to mind. Jodie had said my chocolate pie tasted like it was out of a box and I had made it from scratch using real cocoa. In fact it was far better than the one she brought from T-mart bakery. The PTA would better off without her. She nearly ruined the fall festival putting her two cents in about everybody's booth and her own looked like a rat's nest. But this is too much! Nobody is going to attack my daughter and get away with it. I'll call her right now and tell her a thing or two.

243-2845......what will she say? Just let her have it! That Sherry was well trained in hurting others just like her mother. Like Popeye, *I've had all I can stands and I can't stands no more!* and I will not sit still for my daughter to be harassed! Her daughter is a smarty pants just like her mother! Does she know that her tongue wags at both ends and now her daughter has the same floppiness? Well, that might be a little overboard.

Let's see now. They are not Christians and I am. I want my daughter to be a Christian. In fact I want them to be Christians. Do I really want Marianne to turn the other cheek? It seems my daughter spewed out a few words of her own. What can I say or do to help my daughter?

Write It From Your Heart ♥ Remember a time when words surprised you. _____

_____

_____

_____

_____

_____

_____

_____

_____

_____

_____

_____

_____

_____

_____

_____

_____

_____

Mama's Cooking With Heart ♥
Biscuits

6 cups Martha White self-rising flour

½ cup lard

some milk

Place about six cups of flour in a large mixing bowl. With your clean hand make an indention in the center. In the indention, place a handful of lard, or if you want to use tools then about one-half cup. Use your hand to mix flour with lard adding milk as you go. Continue mixing until at least half the flour, lard and milk combine to make a soft blob of dough. Place more flour on an open space on your counter…or you may use a pastry cloth….then pour the soft dough on the flour. Use your hand to press the dough into the flour a bit, fold it over and press again (knead). Continue to knead until the dough is a soft ball. Dust your rolling pin with flour and roll across the dough until it spreads out to one half-inch thickness. Use your biscuit cutter or an upturned small glass to cut out circles of dough. Place the circles (biscuits) on a greased or ungreased baking pan. Place in a hot oven, about 450 degrees, and wait. Cover the bowl with the unused flour and put away until morning to use again. Keep checking after about 10 minutes and when the biscuits are golden brown, remove from the oven and call, "Breakfast!"

Practice for a few years and you will automatically have the touch.

Biscuit Dough Hoe Cakes

Take biscuit dough and pat out small cakes. Fry in small amount of bacon grease. Watch carefully and turn when the bottom is brown. More grease may need to be added if you have more than one batch to fry. Good cooked over a camp fire in front of your tent.

MAMA SAID LISTEN TO THE BIBLE

Family Heartstrums ♥

"Come on, everybody. Be quiet now, I'm going to read the Bible" were the words we heard before bedtime every single night of our lives of our growing up years. Here we came crowding in on the couch or chairs to listen. The nice big Bible, bought from a door-to-door salesman, rested on her lap. "In the beginning was the Word, and the Word was with God, and the Word was God." John 1:1 seems to belong to Mama's voice.

When we were young we would gather around her and listen or at least sit quietly and pretend to listen. Even when my brothers, as teenagers, bounded to an upstairs room over our family room, Mama would stand at the door of the narrow stairway of our old country home and call the boys by name, "Dick, Jack" or "Mark, Tommy" according to which sons currently occupied the space up there, "Listen now, I'm going to read." At that point she would read aloud a selection from the Bible.

Her purpose was for God's word to be implanted in our minds every single day, no *matter how busy the day, no matter how tired she might have been, or how disinterested we might have been. That was the part of the day, along with mealtimes, when all of us kids gathered together and, absolutely, the only time when we sat quietly with no squabbling and bickering or laughing and teasing. There was no day of long hard farm work, ballgames, or homework that did not culminate with the quiet, still time of the Scripture being read aloud by Mama.*

Heart of the Matter ♥

The first recorded words spoken by God were quite powerful! They brought the world into existence. The second recorded words God spoke were positive words, "It is good." The first words directed to man were verbal. *Genesis 2:15* He spoke with a voice to Adam, Noah, Abraham, and other patriarchs and then to the prophets telling them how they should live and how He would bless them. Later, inspired writers recorded the spoken words into print so that we may know our unchanging, faithful, loving, yet authoritative God. On Mt. Sinai, the finger of God Himself wrote on tablets of stone the Ten Commandments for the Israelites to read, learn and keep. He directed Moses to speak and write 650 specific commandments for the Israelites. Great promises of His love and care accompanied by warnings of punishments for sin allowed the Israelites to choose behavior according to the outcome....if they paid attention to the information available.

Think of the day that Ezra read the book of the law to the Israelites who had returned from captivity. It had been found after many years and the people were called together in an open space to listen. Emotions erupted and they cried tears. Reading *Nehemiah 8* may bring tears flowing from your eyes as you understand their joy of hearing the word of God combined with the guilt from the neglect of His ordinances and the assurance of His love. Their response was to fall down and worship Him with their faces to the ground.

Who read scripture or a Bible story to you and what story do you remember hearing? _____

_____

_____

Old Testament Precedent

Please read these verses and jot down a key phrase you find relevant and discuss.

Ex. 32:15-16 _____

Deut. 6:9 _____

Deut.10: 2 _____

Deut. 28: 58 _____

Deut. 30: 10 _____

Prov. 7:1-3 _____

Jer.31: 33 _____

Probably you have had a little kiddo back up to you with a book and request, "Read dis." Children who hear the stories of Adam, Noah, Abraham, Moses, to name a few, absorb the fact that God expects obedience, He blesses those who obey, and He punishes those who do not. The experiences of the Israelites show His mercy over and over as He rescues them from unpleasant situations they brought upon themselves and obstacles Satan has set for them. His mighty power and faithfulness to His people is demonstrated consistently through the stories of Daniel, Samson, David, and others too numerous to name in this writing. These stories will excite children just as much as fiction if they are read or told with enthusiasm and expression. There is plenty of violence, romance, intrigue, and heroism in the scriptures to enthrall any rambunctious little boy or girl. The bravery of Deborah, Ruth, Esther, and others reveal to our daughters that God can and will use each of us, girls included. Little boys seem especially adept at mimicking David and Goliath, one swinging an imaginary sword while another shouts out the words of David, *"You come to me with a sword, a spear, and a javelin, but I come to you in the name of the LORD." 1 Sam 17:45*

Reread these stories of the ancients and, for certain, you will notice something that you disregarded in the past or that had slipped your mind. *Rom. 15:4 For whatever things were written before were written for our learning, that we through the patience and comfort of the Scriptures might have hope. NKJV*

What Bible story or visual aid do you remember from your childhood Bible class?

_____

_____

_____

_____

_____

God's nature is unchanging. If children hear of God, Jesus Christ, and the Holy Spirit daily, they are more likely to incorporate Him into their lives. Although we live under the wonderful law of Christ and have the essence of God in Christ, we also gain knowledge of His supremacy by reading of His interactions with the people of Old Testament times. Knowing the Creator gives reason to worship.

Children must be taught to distinguish fact from the fiction that is spread broadly though the media and people around them. "God-like" characteristics crop up in many cartoons and movies designed to appeal to children. It is imperative for adults to enable children to determine truth from fiction and recognize the blasphemy that is built into many stories written for children. (The movie, Hercules, based on the pagan myth, has a trio of nymphs singing "Isn't that the gospel truth".) The attack on Christianity is very prevalent in *so-called* good children's literature today. The only antidote to this poison is the Word. To fight off the darts of Satan, our children must be clothed in the armor of God and trained to use the sword of the Spirit. *Eph 6:16 above all, taking the shield of faith with which you will be able to quench all the fiery darts of the wicked one. 17 And take the helmet of salvation, and the sword of the Spirit, which is the word of God. NKJV*

New Testament Admonition

Please read these scriptures and jot down a phrase that you find meaningful and discuss.

Rom. 10:11, 15_____

Rev.1:3 _____

Mark 12:10_____

John 2:22 _____

2 Tim. 3:15 _____

Rom. 2:13 _____

1 Cor. 14:37 _____

1 Cor. 4:6 _____

1 Tim.3:14-15 _____

Heb. 13:22_____

James 1:21, 25_____

    Only the Bible is absolutely right. Any human being can be wrong, either deliberately or mistakenly. As God has inspired no human since His writing was completed, we cannot put our *total* trust in any human commentary in book form, quarterlies, newspapers, or magazines. Human writings must be compared with the Bible, knowing that if there is any difference then the human author is wrong. Who would dare to change God's word after reading *Rev. 22: 18-19?* How can we fail to teach it after reading *2 Peter 3: 1-2?*

    At a ladies' event, someone was asked to share her favorite verse, but she wisely responded, "I don't know. I haven't read it all yet." There is no best verse, but one that is essential to our faith was spoken after the baptism of Jesus when God spoke aloud and claimed Jesus, *Matt 3:17 And suddenly a voice came from heaven, saying, "This is My beloved Son, in whom I am well pleased. NKJV* Quoting God again, in *Mark 9:7,* the same words are written, but adding, *"...Hear Him!" NKJV*

Look in Matthew, Mark, Luke, and John and choose quotations of Jesus that are especially meaningful to you.

1._____

_____

2._____

_____

3._____

_____

4._____

_____

Suggestion: Copy these verses and mail them to someone you love along with an expression of your love.

Mary and Martha both loved Jesus as did their brother Lazarus. However, when Martha chose to serve Jesus by preparing food for His physical body, Mary pleased Him more when she sat down to listen to His words. Jesus remarked to Martha that Mary "has chosen the good part." *Luke 10:42* What seems important to us may not be essential at all, but His Word always is.

Matthew and John actually saw Jesus! They saw Him eat and sleep; they saw Him walk among people who loved Him and people who hated Him; they saw Him speak and saw Him pray; they saw Him *alive, dead,* and *ALIVE* again. Mark and Luke heard the accounts of Jesus from the apostles and saw the results of the apostles' miracles. They were amazed when the blind could see, the deaf could hear, the lame could walk, and the dead could live by the power God gave to Jesus. These passionate experiences incited the witnesses to tell and to write it, led by the Holy Spirit. They told and wrote it because they knew Jesus was the Son of God and will save *any* who believe and obey. **Only those who know about Jesus *can* believe in Him.** Our neighbors, our enemies, and our children need to know! Children love the story of baby Jesus in every month, not just December. They can grieve over the killing of Jesus and celebrate his resurrection every Sunday, not just during a spring holiday.

Don't we love to get letters from ones we love? Just imagine how the early churches must have felt when a letter from Paul arrived! They gathered with eagerness to hear from the one who had taught them of Jesus and gave them the hope of eternal life. Probably those who were literate reached out to hold the letter in their own hands and see the words, but those who could not read likely wanted to hear it over and over in order to remember the precious words. Can you imagine how one would beg to hear it again, just to be sure she understood it perfectly? If you had been an educated person at that time, wouldn't you have quickly copied that letter more than once so that you could keep one for yourself and another to send to your loved ones? *Now when this epistle is read among you, see that it is read also in the church of the Laodiceans, and that you likewise read the epistle from Laodicea. Col.4:16 NKJV*

A dear man who was an elder in the church could not read, yet he often quoted scripture passages after hearing them read repeatedly by his wife! **Tell of someone you know who has a great faith gained by hearing.** _____

_____

_____

_____

Commitment: I, _____, will take a positive step to embed the word of God in the heart of my children, grandchildren, or any children with whom I have contact.

Write what you will do. _____

_____

_____

Write It On Your Heart ♥ Memory verse: *Psalm 119:16*
I will delight myself in Your statutes; I will not forget Your word.
NKJV

♥ Mama's granddaughter, Dana Johnson says, "God knows what is best -- always. It is clear to me now more than ever."

Take It To Heart ♥ Fictional Dilemma for Listen to the Bible

Nadene ripped open the package and looked at the title…just as she hoped…the newest book by Betty Bradford, romance novelist. Nadene had read all the published books Betty Bradford had written, all that the local library had, and now she had to order them from Amazon rather than wait for the library to get them. She loved her Nook but something about holding a real book in her hand and turning the pages made it seem more personal.

Tonight she would read it, right after she read her Bible. Or, maybe a few pages, right after dinner while the kids took their baths but not get engrossed until they were fully asleep. But on the other hand, she recalled last week when she started reading, it took her firmly in its grasp and the Bible was ignored. No, she wouldn't do that again. God's word is more important than any novel, but she would get a smidgen of that when she read a Bible story to the kids.. And this Christian novel has Bible references, so it's not like she is neglecting it altogether. Oh well, she would work it in… decide after the kids finish their homework, say their prayers and go to sleep. Or maybe a peek.

Write From the Heart ♥ Memory of Bible story that greatly affects you emotionally

_____

_____

_____

_____

_____

_____

_____

_____

Mama's Cooking with Heart ♥

Chocolate Rolls

Biscuit dough

Sugar

Cocoa

Butter

Make biscuit dough with a bit more shortening. Dust your hands with flour, break off a piece and form a small ball. On a floured space, roll out to a thin eight-inch circle. On one half of the circle put a mixture of sugar and cocoa, as much as you like, say one-fourth inch deep but not to the edge. Dot the sugar mixture with small blobs of butter. Fold the empty dough half over the sugared half, forming a semicircle and crimp the edges with a fork. Place in a baking pan in a hot oven. Just watch and see when they are brown. Test to see if it is melted and gooey inside. If so they are done. Serve while still warm. Ummmmm.

Mama's Great-granddaughters Cook ♥ with Heart and Convenience

Pizza by Kat Fortner

First you get some dough out of the refrigerator. Next you spread the cheese from the refrigerator all over it. Then you add pepperoni if you want pepperoni pizza. Last you add what ever topping you would like, like olives, peppers. Dad adds garlic this is really good! (Dad also spreads sauce on crust.)

MAMA SAID SPEAK TO OLD PEOPLE

Family Heartstrums ♥

♫ *"What will he do with me, what will he do with me?" circled my heart and soul as the harmony was smoothed out with Granddaddy's distinctive tenor. Yes, Granddaddy is here, I know it without even seeing him. There he is in Bible class studying or holding his ear forward to catch the sound of the preacher, or down on his knee leading a prayer.*

There he is, as always on Sunday morning, coming down the steps on the right of our small picturesque church building, as I descend the steps on the left. "Hi Granddaddy" doesn't even reach my lips before he reaches out for a hug. Granddaddy's big smile always greets me as I approach his side of the churchyard knowing he will be glad to see me. In his suit coat and broad tie, he appears quite proper, but no more lovable than when he came in from threshing wheat in his sweat soaked khaki work clothes.

Speaking to Granddaddy was in pleasant obedience to Mama's instruction to, "Always speak to Granddaddy. Old people really appreciate having someone speak to them." What a blessing

*it was to have Granddaddy and to be taught
to show respect to him. The tiny bit we know of
our grandmother, Maxie, is from his story of her
pulling the tiny peaches off a tree to see if they
had survived the overnight freeze. He laughed
every time quoting her, "That one made it, that
one made it," until he pointed out that she was
killing them.*

Heart of the Matter ♥

The elderly have earned our respect and attention. Simply living a long time gives them experiences that, if shared with younger people in the proper way, will help them avoid much pain and suffering from mistakes. Younger ones who associate with those that are wise from living a life of dedication to God's word are indeed blessed. Every generation does not have to experience everything personally to know the consequences of many choices and behaviors. Older Christians know that living as God's child brings innumerable blessings and successes in this life in addition to the awesome assurance of heaven in the next one. It is such fun to hear their laughter when they tell the tales of small misdeeds and the consequences endured or the narrow escapes of a day gone by. Many of the elderly have wonderful conversion stories and will happily explain the emotions and actions resulting from learning a truth from the Bible. From Granddaddy we learned that God healed his sore toe when a good ole dog came along to lick the infection out.

What funny advice has an older person given you?

_____

_____

In the early times, people lived hundreds of years, so who knows when old age took hold. If Methuselah lived to be 969 years old, was he old at 900? Noah had three sons after he was 500 years old, so that must have been in his prime time. He built the ark after that, even after his sons grew up and married, so the prime of his life must have continued for 300 more years. But times changed. Abraham lived only 175 years and the Bible says he died at a good old age.

The Patriarchs did not have a retirement. It was a lifetime job. Artists may depict these leaders as being old, having long white beards, but old age to them didn't begin at fifty. When Joshua was eighty-five God suggests he is old but still gives him the mission of allotting the land to Abraham's descendants with the promise that He will drive out the inhabitants of the land. Joshua accepts the responsibility and explains to the people, *"But, the LORD helping me, I will drive them out just as he said." Josh 14:12 NIV*

King David offered to take care of Barzillai, a man of eighty years, because Barzillai had cared for him in the past. Barzillai preferred to stay in his own home, as most elderly people do, and politely refused the king's invitation with these words, "(2 Sam 19:34-37)"*How many more years will I live, that I should go up to Jerusalem with the king? 35 I am now eighty years old. Can I tell the difference between what is good and what is not? Can your servant taste what he eats and drinks? Can I still hear the voices of men and women singers? Why should your servant be an added burden to my lord the king? 36 Your servant will cross over the Jordan with the king for a short distance, but why should the king reward me in this way? 37 Let your servant return, that I may die in my own town near the tomb of my father and mother"* NIV

Tell of some task an elderly person still performs well.

_____

_____

_____

_____

Old Testament Precedent

Please read these verses and jot down a key phrase you find relevant and discuss.

Lev. 19:32_____

Job 12:12_____

Prov. 17:6_____

Ps. 71:9_____

Prov. 23:22_____

Isa. 46:4_____

Prov. 10:27_____

Prov. 16:31_____

Prov. 20:29_____

Gen. 45:9-11_____

Assuming that scholars of history are correct, John escaped the death of a martyr as suffered by most of the apostles, but he did suffer exile to a lonely island. This being true, he would have been an old man when God sent to him the revelation of Jesus Christ with the instructions to write it down and send it to churches. John, once designated as a "son of thunder" in his younger days can now be called "son of comfort." Knowing the extreme suffering of Christians, John was chosen to give them a message of hope. The suffering is temporary! God knows what they are suffering and has a plan to reward them. The reward will be so wonderful that it can only be described to mortals in comparisons, "like untos". John writes to the Christians that Jesus will come for them, He will defeat Satan and his followers, and He will welcome them to endless joy. He writes that Jesus will wipe away their tears!

New Testament Admonition

Please read these verses and jot down a key phrase you find relevant and discuss.

1Tim. 5:9-10_____

1Tim. 5:1-2_____

Titus 2:2-3_____

Luke 1:18_____

Anna, a prophetess of great age, and Simeon were both in the temple area when baby Jesus was brought to the temple. Both recognized Him as the promised Messiah and declared Him as such. Don't you know Mary and Joseph were delighted and astonished at this announcement about the One who seemed liked like an ordinary baby boy? Of course, they had been told by an angel, no less, but some things are just too awesome to fully understand, even when they happen to us. This recognition of the Son of God was given to a couple of elderly people who were expecting God to keep His promise. The Bible does not state that Simeon was elderly but it does say he had been promised not to die until he had seen the Lord's Christ.

Older Christians today, though they have not suffered physical torture (at least in the United States), are all feeling the ravages that a long life on a temporary earth bestows. Diminished hearing can lead to loneliness, even in a group, if the conversation is limited to those with acute hearing. Arthritis crooks the bones, twists the limbs, and inflames the muscles sending constant pain to some. Weak bones break easily and mend slowly. Aches and pains cause some to complain and explain their discomforts to excess.

A diminished memory causes childhood stories to be repeated, and repeated, and repeated. Mistakes in ordinary household and personal chores result in dangers, which in domino effect, result in a gradual loss of independence and freedom to live in their own home. When the car keys are taken, many experience an almost unbearable sense of being mistreated, of being in prison! Loneliness and the grief of losing a beloved spouse, dear friends, and family are often cause of depression. Some choose to suffer alone rather than be a burden on family and friends. How great the longing for heaven must be for those dear ones! No more pain, no more death, always light, living with perfection! What wonderful hope John the Comforter gives them! Jesus knows and will come for them!

In this century, humanity is expected to live much longer due to medical advances in fighting diseases and aiding the body to repair itself after an accident. God has blessed America with plenty of healthy food, clean water, and comfortable living conditions. Books, magazines, and television shows are crammed with good advice about keeping our bodies well and capable of movement to a more advanced age. Because of these blessings, more elderly people are among us and we can reasonably expect to live longer than our ancestors did. Of course, no one knows when the Lord may come for us or when any life may end. Maybe you have noticed that people reaching their seventies no longer look ancient. God's blessing of better health care and good health practices are making a difference in longevity and the physical appearance of the elderly.

Some churches have programs to honor and enrich the lives of the older people in the congregation. Some provide transportation to the church services for those who no longer drive or feel unsafe driving at night. Trips are planned to various restaurants or interesting places to provide the opportunity of the elderly to enjoy the company of one another and to give a different experience from the family. Banquets and other avenues of recognition attempt to express the appreciation and love of the congregation.

None of the special activities take the place of a hug, phone call, a caring note, or any of the day to day expressions of love and appreciation. One to one, personal attention is needed. If we appreciate the wisdom and joy these precious ones give and are thankful for their past contributions, the attention needed by them will not be a heavy burden. Elderly people, for the most part, are on fixed income and many deny themselves even small luxuries. Frugality may be necessary in order to maintain a decent place to live, appropriate medication, and adequate food. Many are careful not to burden their family with requests for help or transportation beyond what is absolutely necessary. Even those who are financially secure benefit from the gift of time spent in conversation or a small gift that indicates that someone loves them.

Name an older person that you hold in especially high esteem and tell why.

_____

_____

_____

_____

_____

_____

_____

_____

_____

Suggest five things one might do to brighten the life of an older person.

1._____

2._____

3._____

4._____

5._____

Think of an older person that you find distant, grouchy, inconsiderate, or otherwise less congenial and plan a kind action you will take.

_____

_____

_____

_____

Commitment: I,_____, will help (a child)_____ do a kindness for (elderly person) _____.

Write It On Your Heart ♥ *Memory verse: Isa 46:4 Even to your old age, I am He, And even to gray hairs I will carry you! I have made, and I will bear; Even I will carry, and will deliver you. NKJV*

♥ *Mama's granddaughter, KaRen Coffman says,* "Speaking to old people benefits everyone! I think that the older my parents and I get the more this seems important. There is a wealth in older people, a wealth of knowledge of life and love. We need to show them the respect they have earned and someday we, hopefully, will have earned."

Take It To Heart ♥ Dilemma for Speak to Old People

Jaisy was in such a hurry…first to pick up Kasi at school and then to get the brownies made for the little league bake sale. There was always something going on and then there was Grannie hovering in the back of her mind. Jaisy had not seen her in a month and her cell phone said she had missed her phone call, but she just did not have time to call her back. Well, she had seen her from a distance across the parking lot at church but she had been in a hurry to get home and make some calls for her neighborhood watch program. Next month she would make time for Grannie, even spend an afternoon with her.

Even as she darted into the school parking lot and loaded up the kids, she noticed the text message signal was humming but she ignored it. "Hey, Sugar, get your seatbelt fastened. We have to finish your home-work before Steve's game. It's an afternoon game today so we don't have much time. There's that phone again….looks like it's from Mom. I'll pull over here. Mom doesn't *ever* call at this time of day".

Jaisy cautiously pulled her van into a parking space and opened her phone. "Mom, what's up?" Tears rolled slowly over her cheeks and dripped on her new blouse, as she said, "Mom, what can I do? Should I come right now? But I have the kids….she may not last the night? Oh, Mom…how can I be in two places at once? Jason is at the new job site…He can't leave…. Will she know if I come or not? Do you need me, Mom?"

_____

_____

_____

_____

_____

Write From the Heart ♥ Memory of a time spent with a grandparent or elderly one.

_____

_____

_____

_____

_____

_____

_____

_____

_____

_____

_____

_____

_____

_____

_____

_____

_____

_____

_____

_____

_____

_____

_____

_____

Mama's Cooking With Heart ♥

Peach Cobbler

Go running out when you hear Granddaddy's truck pull into the yard and see the pinkish yellow peaches piled in bushel baskets. Watch Mama pick out the basket she wants and follow into the house, breathing in the freshness, the sweetness, the goodness of ripe peaches. Take the one Mama peels for you and eat, licking the drips of juice off your hands. Eat another one if she will let you.

Peel, pit, and slice about 8 ripe peaches into 8 to 10 slices. Line a metal baking pan with pastry, pressing in more dough to patch any holes that appear. Mix about 1/3 cup of flour into 2 cups of sugar. Pour sugar mixture over peaches and stir until every slice is coated.

Don't worry: juice will come from peaches and sugar will melt. Cut several pieces of butter randomly around in the peaches. Place another layer of pastry over the top and seal the edges to the pastry coming up the sides of the pan. Cut a few slits in the top pastry. Sprinkle top with a pretty good layer of sugar and dot with butter.

Bake at 350 degrees quite a while, watching to see when the top is brown in the spots where the butter isn't. Be patient till Daddy comes in at noon for dinner.

Mama's Great-granddaughters Cook ♥
with Heart and Convenience

Noodles by Addie Fortner

First you get one of the packages. Open the cabinet and then there is a pan in it. You have to put the hotish, coldish, warm water in it. Then you put the timer on it. Wait for it to bubble really good. Then you're supposed to wash your hands and then you put the noodles in. Then you are supposed to get them out and pour most of the water out and then you eat it.

When you put the noodle in you have to rub it with a fork so the bubbles won't break.

There's a special packet in it, well, you have to dump it in before you eat it.

Invite a young child you love to dictate to you a recipe she has watched or helped you make.

_____

_____

_____

_____

_____

_____

_____

_____

_____

_____

_____

MAMA SAID MIND YOUR MAMA AND DADDY

Family Heartstrums ♥

As Mark tossed the ball over Tommy's head to sink the basketball into the hoop, Daddy's voice ended the game. "Let's go boys," he boomed. After another quick scramble, off they went to the hot, itchy hay field. In the summer the entire day was filled with work, until late afternoon when they could skinny dip in the creek deep hole to cool off and rid themselves of sweat, dust, and chaff. No arguing or delaying....but for a moment. Daddy said it; they did it.

"Obey your parents in the Lord" was probably the first verse we ever learned from the Bible due to Mama's repetition. It was needed. Along with "Honor your father and mother", it probably was the verse heard most often. Whether we wanted to or not, we were to obey Daddy and Mama, which was the part of "honor" that was most stressed to us kids. Not that we always did. It was difficult to comply with "stop aggravating" one another and we never did get that one down pat.

The consequence of disobedience to Daddy was sure and prompt, with no jury trial. We didn't *always enjoy our duties but they were an essential part of being a farm family and instilled in us a work ethic. My brothers climbed aboard the tractor at a young age, loving to drive and "be a man". When Daddy laid out the plan for the day, it was not up for discussion or debate. The milking, the plowing, the haying, the planting and on, and on, and on had to be accomplished if the family had food, shelter and clothing, and Daddy couldn't do it all. The girls took on the woman's work in the same way. Part of honoring one's parents as a young person is cooperating in the necessary family tasks, not just on Father's Day and Mother's Day.*

Heart of the Matter ♥

Granddaddy also taught us to be respectful of Mama. He would tell us, with prejudice of course, "You've got the best mama in the world," hoping we would treat her in such a way.   She, in turn, thought she had the best daddy in the world and her example of respect and love for him was evident. Even when times were hard and roads were long and narrow, two or three times a year Daddy traveled a three hour drive back 'home' to the steep hills of northern Tennessee to visit "Pap" and Miss Alice, his stepmother. Parents are never too old or disabled to need attention from their loved ones. Parents may be financially secure and able to hire employees to supply their physical needs, but the affection of their family cannot be purchased. Respect and honor are priceless, more valuable than gold, yet are usually freely given.

All of us have seen miserable children who did not obey, honor, or respect their parents. Why? They were not trained to do so. Parents who allow children to disobey and talk disrespectfully are not doing that child a favor, but rather are contributing to the child's unhappiness. Little tykes who rule the household and have no boundaries will become teenagers who have little respect for any authority, including their parents. Without proper training these teenagers will go on to be selfish adults with disregard for the needs of others as well as their aging parents. It begins with teaching Bible principles. Trouble is sure when God's advice is disregarded.

Tell one incident that showed how your parents honored your grandparents.

_____

_____

_____

In the age of the patriarchs the father's word was law. No doubt Noah ruled his family well, as his wife, his sons and their wives were the only ones saved from a world overrun with sin. *Gen. 9* In contrast, Eli tumbled over backward and died upon receiving the news of Israel's losing a battle in which his two disobedient sons were killed. *1 Sam. 2:12, 1 Sam. 3:17-18* When Ruth cared for her mother-in-law, Naomi, and took Naomi's God as her own, she became the grandmother of King David and an ancestor of Jesus, our Savior. *Ruth, Matthew 1:5*

Old Testament Precedent

Please read these verses and jot down a key phrase you find relevant and discuss.

Ex. 20:12 _____

Prov. 31:28 _____

Mal. 1:6_____

Ex. 21:15 _____

Lev. 19:3_____

Deut. 21:18-21 _____

Deut. 27:16_____

Prov. 1:8_____

Prov. 15:20 _____

Prov. 23:22 _____

Why should our children honor us? Because the Bible says so. What can we do to make that command a positive one, to recognize it as a blessing and not a hardship? To state the obvious, *we can be honorable.* We should model the characteristics that are honorable: honesty, concern for others, kindness, gentleness, reverence for God and His Son, and good humor. Who wants to spend time with a grouch? Rare is the person inclined to be kind to someone selfish or harsh. Each generation must model the behavior that is desired for the next generation.

If parents have been negligent or hurtful to their children, the command may be difficult, but if we remember that Jesus obeyed even when it was difficult, then our obedience is possible. Remember in Gethsemane Jesus prayed in agony. *Luke 22:44* In all things we can go to Him for the perfect pattern. If the parents in a family do not behave rationally or Godly, then honoring them may be difficult and take the form of extending kindness to them without necessarily spending time with them. Unfortunately, we know that drugs, including alcohol, have ruined some parents, so children who survive such an environment must struggle and pray in order to be kind and respectful to parents who let them down. Victims of incest or rape by a parent's 'lover' will only, by the power of forgiveness, (discussed in another lesson), be able to obey this command to honor.

Such tragedies are prevalent. Check with your local school counselor or rape crisis center for statistics in your area. Such parents do not deserve an emotional attachment and a physical distancing may be required to be safe and healthy, but adult sons and daughters still may show honor and respect by treating the harmful parent kindly from a distance and praying for their repentance. Sadly, adult children of ungodly parents must protect their own children from emotional and physical harm that might result from personal contact with those grandparents.

Touching our hearts especially, we remember Jesus hanging in agony with the sins of the world upon Him, yet having the foresight to pass the care of his mother on to his beloved disciple, John. How can we do less? Yet many do. Nursing homes are filled with those whose families are too busy to care for them. The nursing home route is easier, and in some cases, the best choice. Thankfully, in our country, wonderful skilled care facilities are available for the elderly when they became needful of round the clock care. Such facilities provide assistance in physical care along with respect and kindness but can never substitute for the loving attention required from family. Many residents in elder care facilities do not receive the honor they need from their family, but spend lonely days feeling forgotten by those they brought into the world and nurtured through childhood. Loved ones of patients in residential care should visit at unanticipated times to make sure the care is consistent and that needs are met promptly.

In some cases, children must assist their parents financially and for a Christian to disregard this duty would be hypocritical as Jesus taught. *Matt. 15:4-6* Parents who provided for the children are entitled to the similar favor. Those able and willing to care for an elderly parent or in-law in their home deserve much admiration! The job of caring for someone who may be ill or disabled may appear to be a thankless job, in some cases, but it is definitely temporary, and our Lord sees. No one yet has escaped the discomforts of old age except by dying, and we won't either.

Write three things you would say to your parent if you could see them today. If your parent is still living, say it face to face. A card with your own handwriting and message will be a treasure that can be read and reread.

1_____

2._____

3_____

New Testament Admonition

Please read these verses and jot down a key phrase you find relevant and discuss.

Luke 2:51_____

Rom. 1:30-32_____

Eph.6:1-2_____

1 Tim. 5:1-5_____

Matt 15:4-6_____

"Yes, Sir, Yes, Ma'am" may be currently out of style in many environments but is music to the ears in our southern states. Mr. and Mrs. are titles that are seldom heard except in some schools. Children seldom give seats to parents or even grandparents when they enter a room. Some of our simple good manners of recent yesteryear that showed regard for parents have been tossed in the litter bin. Who eats first these days? The children are certainly not waiting for the second table when guests are present. Most adults of this generation (including the writer) and in our country would be miserable eating while a hungry child waited. When parents give in to children who push, shove, whine, hit, sulk etc. in order to get their way regardless of the situation, the child does not learn to honor, respect, or obey the parent.

Some adults find it difficult to require a child to show respect to themselves and other adults when the customs have changed so radically. Yet, basic courtesy never goes out of style, so teaching basic good manners is an excellent starting point. One person should speak at the time, especially if a parent is speaking. Holding a door open is a thoughtful, considerate thing to do. "Thank you" is an appreciated response. Happiness may be a choice but obedience should not be! One parent should ensure that the other is honored, yes, on Mother's Day and Father's Day, but that is only the minutest minimum! Grandmothers just beam when little grandsons bring in flowers to them or their mom. Grandparents are delighted when granddaughters say, "kank you" when given her juice sippy and can hardly resist a request accompanied by "please".

Modeling, the most powerful of all teaching tools, is a compelling, effective method. "Train up" is the Bible phrase that involves modeling at its core. A child who knows how to behave and has discipline and self-control feels more secure in every circumstance and will honor their parents as a result.

Write about a time when good manners were required in your childhood.

_____

_____

_____

_____

_____

Jesus, as a child, set the perfect example. When He was taken to Jerusalem to the temple for the first time, He involved himself so deeply with the Jewish scholars that He was apparently unaware when Mary and Joseph started home without Him. After a day's travel, and discovering that Jesus was not in the company of travelers, back they went to Jerusalem and searched for three days before finding Him in the temple where He had been all along. As an explanation to His mother, He asked, "Didn't you know I would be about My Father's business?" He returned to Nazareth with them, however, and continued in subjection to His mother and stepfather. *Luke 2:41-52*

Commitment: I, _____, will teach words of good manners and respect for _____ to _____.

How will you do this? _____
_____
_____

Write It On Your Heart ♥ Memory verse: *John 14:10 Do you not believe that I am in the Father, and the Father in Me? The words that I speak to you I do not speak on My own authority; but the Father who dwells in Me does the works. NKJV*

♥Mama's granddaughter, Tracy Edmonson says, "Even though I never met my grandmother, I can know what was important to her by looking at her children's values. Strong faith keeps rolling down through the generations. It is even more special to me because I don't remember my father who died when I was two, but I can see how she influenced my aunts and uncles."

Take It to Heart ♥ Fictional Dilemma for Mind Your Mama and Daddy

"Sherry, it's time for me to take you home," Jan had reluctantly urged. "Your homework is finished and that's what Mom said we may do together. I need to get back and fix Tom's supper."

"It's OK for me to stay a little longer. Mr. Tom likes for me to be here. He says I'm funny," argued Sherry mildly as she did five days a week and after church on Sunday. But Jan couldn't give in; she knew the consequences. If she allowed Sherry to stay too long, it might be two weeks before her mom allowed her to jump on the Neighborhood Kids church bus again.

How could Sherry want to go home when her mother is zonked out on the couch and a filthy kitchen is waiting for her to clean up? Movie after movie, smoke after smoke, beer after beer was the life of that house. Jan could barely breathe when she went inside the tiny apartment to get permission to take Sherry on an outing of any sort. And to think, life could be so different for Sherry with a few different choices.

But for now, Jan was so confused. How could she teach Sherry to honor her father and mother when they lived such a dishonorable life? Well, she really couldn't say much about the father as he never entered the picture except in Sherry's fantasies. But the mother was alive and well and very much in the picture, on the couch, calling the shots of Sherry's comings and goings and cashing the government checks. God didn't say just honor the honorable, but how?

_____

_____

_____

_____

_____

Write it From the Heart♥ Memory of your parents or care-takers

_____

_____

_____

_____

_____

_____

_____

_____

_____

_____

_____

_____

_____

_____

_____

_____

_____

_____

_____

_____

_____

_____

_____

_____

_____

_____

_____

_____

Mama's Cooking With Heart ♥
Fried Chicken

Small fryer chicken
Salt
Flour
Lard

In early spring, order 30 baby chickens. When they come, with little heads peeking out of round holes in the box, place them in a brooder warmed by a light bulb. Feed them crushed corn until they are big enough to leave the brooder. As they grow little wing feathers and become as big as your hand, let them loose in the chicken yard but continue to feed them every day. Finally, when they have grown as large as a football, it's time to......ooooo, I'm not telling that part! Go on the Internet and find out.

Salt the chicken pieces and dredge in flour. Place in a skillet that has lots of hot grease. Watch. If it gets too hot it will burn on the outside and be raw on the inside…so start off hot and turn down the heat and let it cook. Turn each piece as it browns on the skillet side so the other side can cook. Remove each piece when it is cooked to the firm stage…a toothpick will slip right in…and place on a platter. Call, "Dinner's ready!"

Write a recipe or cooking story from your childhood.

_____

_____

_____

_____

_____

_____

_____

_____

_____

_____

_____

Mama's Great-granddaughters Cook ♥ with Heart and Convenience

Quick Take Chicken Parmesan that my mom showed me for my twin sons by Meggan Brant

A pack of the pre-cooked breaded chicken patties or breast tenders

1 jar of favorite spaghetti sauce

1 pkg. shredded Italian and/or mozzarella cheese

Preheat oven to chicken package directions. In a baking dish, lay desired amount of chicken pieces. Pour spaghetti sauce over the tops, almost covering them all. Sprinkle with cheese- however little or lot you want. Bake following package directions.

In the meantime, boil spaghetti. Add in some garlic bread to the oven and in about 25-30 minutes you have a delicious chicken Parmesan! Cooper calls it "Momma make the chicken with the red sauce" and Eli agrees.

MAMA SAID KEEP YOUR GOOD NAME

Family Heartstrums ♥

"Oh, are you Louise's daughter?"

"Yes, Ma'am."

"She is the sweetest thing!"

Many conversations began with remarks similar to that. How did my behavior jive with Mama's good name? Hiding behind her skirts probably earned the label of shy. Playing with brothers probably earned the "tomboy" label. None of us kids overtly intended to embarrass or bring shame to the family name so we were happy being known as a Massey, or as a sibling to one another. Mama wanted us to behave in a way that would bring honor to God, as well as the family, therefore, she was delighted when a friend spoke well of us kids.

My brothers, Jack and Mark, still laugh when they tell of one schoolmate who acted in a way that brought him lots of attention, but not admiration. It seemed the poor guy would lick the soles of his shoes to show he would do something no one else would do. Fortunately the boy lived in the "burg" and had not been *stomping around the barn as had my brothers.*

Siblings often label one another in descriptive or insulting ways we may not want to remember. Many families have a smart kid, a kind one, a loner, a fighter, a helpful kid, or a blabber mouth. I always wanted to be like my older sister because I heard Daddy refer to her as "classy" and Mama called her "smart". But all of us were Masseys, and that should mean honorable.

Heart of the Matter ♥

Unfortunately, some parents have been heard to say, "You're just like Uncle Jed…lazy to the bone." Parents should guard against labeling a child negatively because a child is inclined to behave accordingly, believing the label as a prediction. Also, searching for his own individuality, one child may adopt a negative role assuming that the positive one has been taken by another. Every child deserves to be loved and labeled with an endearment or affectionate nickname.

"Don't lose your good reputation" or "You need to keep your good name" was a reminder that something priceless can be lost by behavior. A good reputation is very difficult to retrieve and or build if the neighborhood continues to speak of dishonorable behavior. Years past the event, some will remember misbehavior and cling to negative thoughts about a person's character, believing the leopard can not lose its spots. Only with repentance and purposeful change of behavior can a reputation be cleaned up. It is very pleasant to hear of someone who is really different from the reputation earned by sowing wild oats.

The Bible says a good name is better than great riches. *Prov. 22:1* Just as a good reputation can be lost, a kind deed is often recalled and reported. Children often remember with fondness the person who helped them learn a skill, helped them out of a difficulty, or even gave them a piece of gum. When someone asks if an acquaintance with the same last name is related, one tends to wonder about the character of that person. We ponder if that person brings honor or dishonor to the name. We tend to ask ourselves if the "relative" will bring favor or disfavor to our own by association.

Mothers often emphasize that the actions of each person in a family reflect on the other members, especially the *mother*. Around our house, *lazy, dishonest,* or *immoral* were descriptions that amounted to *sorry.* Each time someone inquired if I were Louise's daughter, I assumed they were recalling something admirable about her and hoped that the light of her good name would shine on me. Think of the pleasant emotions that arise each time that someone happily introduces you, claiming you as relative.

Remember an eccentric or notable character in the community of your childhood you will never forget because of his/her reputation. _____

_____

_____

_____

When Cain was confronted by God after murdering Abel, he thought that the punishment of being a fugitive and a vagabond was more than he could bear. As a result, a mark was placed upon his head that prevented anyone from slaying him but the same mark also announced to the world that this man was a murderer of his brother. *Gen. 4:15* His reputation was shot! Compare that with the reputation of Job. When Satan mulled over Job and could find no fault with him, the devil accused God of shielding him. *Job 1* Samson evidently had three reputations, one as a ladies' man which led to his capture, another as strong warrior, and finally as a mighty defender of God's chosen people. The consequence he suffered for his spiritual weakness resulted in his physical weakness, blindness, capture, and slavery to the Philistines. He persevered, however, and when God renewed his strength, he sacrificed his own life to bring down the building upon the leaders of Israel's enemies.

Daniel, Shadrach, Meshach, and Abednego had such superb reputations that the co-workers were jealous and attempted to kill them, but God protected them, resulting in the king's admiration and reward. Deborah's reputation of being powerful and having wisdom from God was such that the captain of her army refused to go to a certain battle without her. *Judges 4* Joseph's reputation as being an accurate dream interpreter sprang him from the Egyptian jail into Pharaoh's palace. *Gen. 41* The reputation of the Israelites traveled faster than they did. Some of the inhabitants of the Promised Land fled before them because they heard that this people had a God who fought *for* them.

Prov. 20:11 Even a child is known by his deeds, whether what he does is pure and right. NKJV Every child has a reputation even at a young age.....a good baby, content, fussy, crier, and at a later date, well behaved, good manners, "all boy", feisty, bossy, bully, timid, dependable, etc. In schools, teachers hear of the troubled children even before they have them in their classroom. The wise teacher will ignore the reputation of such a student and give the benefit of the doubt. Students behave differently from teacher to teacher or may have matured. Just in case the reputation might not be justified, allowing the child to have a new beginning without a negative reputation is a blessing.

Likewise, some teachers earn a reputation of cruelty or kindness, apt at teaching or inept, motivating or discouraging, which causes some students to avoid them or select them if possible. One student who suffered mightily in the classroom nicknamed his teacher, "Goat-tail", supposedly because of her chopped-off hair rather than their head-butting episodes. **Remember a time when your parent reminded you of the family name and your obligation to it.**

_____

_____

_____

_____

Old Testament Precedent

Please read these verses and jot down a key phrase you find relevant and discuss.

Gen. 12:2_____

 2 Sam. 7:9-10_____

2 Sam. 23:18_____

1 Kings 1:47_____

Eccl. 7:1_____

Prov. 25:9-10_____

Esther 9:3-5 _____

2 Chronicles 26:14-16 _____

The reputation of the Nazarenes was so bad that when Nathaniel heard that Jesus was from there, he said, "Can anything good come out of Nazareth?" Yet, Jesus' reputation as a healer spread far and wide and multitudes came to see him. One woman even thought if she managed to touch His clothes she would be healed. Because of this same wonderful reputation, the Jewish leaders were jealous and planned his murder. Jesus also told of being mislabeled by those attempting to find fault, saying in *Luke 7:34 The Son of Man came eating and drinking, and you say, 'Here is a glutton and a drunkard, a friend of tax collectors and "sinners." NIV*

Ananias had heard of ***that Saul***!! the one who persecuted Christians. So at first he had second thoughts about going to the street where God wanted him to meet with Saul. But God explained that He had plans for Saul so Ananias obeyed and Saul became the apostle Paul. Paul remained zealous, but after his conversion, he directed his zeal for God through his Son, Jesus Christ.

Dorcas came back to her own wake! Dorcas had earned the reputation of being generous as well as being a good seamstress. The recipients of her products grieved at her death and showed the clothes she had made. What would you find if you could listen in while others remember you?

New Testament Admonition

Please read these verses and jot down a key phrase you find relevant and discuss.

Acts 6:3_____

Acts 10:22_____

Gal. 2:2_____

Phil.2:5-7_____

Rom. 16:19_____

1 Cor. 5:11-12_____

Acts 17:6_____

1 Tim. 3:7_____

3 John 4_____

Acts 22:12_____

If our spiritual family is known in the community by the way we behave, what will be the reputation of the church in your community? Will it be known as a family of generous, caring people? Will it be known as moral and honest? Will it be known as Christ-like?

If Christ is living in us, what reputation must we have? A true Christian will soon be known for the kind encouraging words, for helpful actions, and for a merciful and generous caring nature. A true Christian will be known to have a clean mind and reverence for God. We should memorize the fruits of the spirit and behave in such a way that those characteristics will be a part of our reputation.

Without naming names, tell of a time when you have been embarrassed by someone who claims to be a member of His church but does not act Christ-like.

_____

_____

_____

Matt 5:16 Let your light so shine before men, that they may see your good works and glorify your Father in heaven. NKJV

List three things you can do that will enhance the reputation of your church family in your community.

_____

_____

_____

As our children look to us as models, we must make sure the adjectives attached to our names are righteous ones. Knowing they will follow in our steps, we should stress the positive traits and describe them in terms that give them positive feelings. A four-year-old once told her grandmother, "Thank you" for calling her Sweetheart. Some adults playfully call their beloved children "Stinkers" but does the child always know that the person really thinks he's a sweetie?

The language a child uses is the same language of their family. If rudeness and foul language flow from a young child's mouth, everyone knows the child did not create the words, he simply repeats what he has heard. Creative older children may invent rude retorts and descriptive names on their own unless they are not taught by instruction and example to speak with respect. One five year old asked his mother, "*Hypothetically*, what would happen if I had to pull a card?" referring to a discipline measure in kindergarten. Imitating and repeating a language is a child's expert way of learning.

Children who are bullied may very well become bullies when they are in the company of smaller children, but children who experience kindness and reason will become the peacemakers. Although we encourage our children to be courageous and experience different activities, we do not want them to become daredevils or careless.

Group activity: Describe the reputation of someone in your congregation and let others guess the identity. Keep it positive, please.

_____

_____

_____

If you have one word inscribed on your tombstone labeling your reputation, what will it be? _____

I, _____, will encourage _____to earn and keep a good reputation.

 How will you do this? _____

_____

_____

Write It On Your Heart ♥   Memory verse: Ps 89:1 *I will sing of the mercies of the LORD forever; With my mouth will I make known Your faithfulness to all generations. NKJV*

♥ Mama's granddaughter, Tracy Edmonson says, "Knowing that my family before me lived a Godly life is one of the greatest gifts I've ever been given. I know there are many, many people who aren't fortunate enough to say that, so I never take that gift for granted. I thank God for my Christian heritage and pray that I and my descendants can preserve it. "

Take it to Heart ♥ Fictional Dilemma for Keep Your Good Name

That lady coming in is no lady. She may come this way, to my pew. Her skirt is slit way too high and she knows it. Why is she coming in here anyway? Maybe to flirt with the men. But maybe not. Jesus told the woman actually caught red-handed in adultery to "go and sin no more"….maybe she has changed, or wants to change. If she is coming to worship, she should have dressed better!

Do I speak to her and have everyone think she is my friend? Jesus ate with publicans and sinners, but I am not nearly as good as He, and He knew what to say and I don't.   What will I say? She looks pretty in spite of being a little on the sleazy side…the teen girls may try to look like that…after all those boys are looking her over. She's coming, she's looking right at me and there is an empty seat right here….so I have to do something right now! What should I do? _____

_____

_____

_____

_____

_____

Write It From the Heart ♥ Memory relating to your family's good name.

_____

_____

_____

_____

_____

_____

_____

_____

_____

_____

_____

_____

_____

_____

_____

_____

_____

Mama's Cooking With Heart ♥
Potatoes

Cut potato into parts making sure that each part has an eye. Plant into prepared garden soil. Wait, wait, wait. Dig under the large green bushy vine and find lots of new potatoes where you had planted only a part. Tell God thank you.

New Potatoes

Wash small new potatoes thoroughly; boil in the peeling until tender. On your plate, open, add butter and salt to taste. Also may be cooked in a pot of fresh green beans.

Large potatoes:

Fried Potatoes: Peel each potato, cut into strips or cubes. Heat a skillet with a chunk of lard or bacon grease, a little or a lot, and place potatoes in very carefully. Watch and turn occasionally with a metal egg turner. Remove them from the skillet when the potatoes are soft or brown and crispy, your choice. Place potatoes on a napkin to absorb the excess grease and then transfer them to a serving dish. Add salt before or after cooking. Leftovers from breakfast are good between a cold biscuit for an after school snack.

Mama's Great-granddaughters Cook ♥ with Heart and Convenience

Peanut Butter Krispy Balls by Shelby Fortner

Need:

1 stick of butter

1 cup of peanut butter

2 cups of powdered sugar

2 1/3 - 3 cups of Rice Krispies

First you need to soften the butter; around 5 - 10 seconds (in microwave). After that, add your peanut butter and powdered sugar with it. (Using a mixer on High) After that, put in the Rice Krispies and they're ready to eat! (DO NOT HEAT)

Invite a sweet young lady to write a no-bake dessert recipe.

_____

_____

_____

_____

_____

_____

_____

_____

_____

_____

_____

_____

MAMA SAID DON'T TELL STORIES (LIES)

Family Heartstrums♥

"Liar!" I accused Jack, who evidently loved to hear me scream. "He said I can't do a chin-up, but I can and he knows it! I just did it but he said I didn't do it right!"

"Max, don't call him a liar! He is just teasing. If you will just hush and pay him no attention, he'll stop teasing you. He just wants to make you fuss." So Jack wasn't in trouble, at least not as much as I, because he was just teasing, as usual! In spite of Jack's sly grin, I had no choice but to go outside and prove again I really could chin myself on the low limb of the tree. He is the one who showed me how to do it in the first place. He thinks his muscles are bigger just because he's a boy. He is just a story teller!

Mama didn't tolerate lying, so "Don't tell stories" was imbedded in our psyche and included the fact that liars will not be in heaven. We were not to even call one another "that word". Our preachers explained in vivid terms where we would be if we don't make

*it to heaven so I tended to believe that such
a clear choice would be made by everyone.
Eventually it became evident that the world is
well supplied with liars, uh, story tellers.*

Heart of the Matter ♥

What an example is being set by people of the world! The politicians each call their opponent a liar and then proceed to prove it. Occasionally one may admit to having "misspoken". Commercials tout products that do not produce the result advertised. Even preachers have been exposed for having adulterous relationships that were concealed by lies to their wives, families, and church. Children's television programs and movies now show children lying to get their way or to disguise some other misbehavior without reaping any chastisement for it. Children learn to lie when it is successful. They get out of trouble, they get what they want, or someone thinks it's funny. Success! Examples are set by parents who are "not at home" when they don't want to talk on the phone, "already have plans" when they don't want to accept an invitation, fudge a bit on the income tax, etc. The comedy line on most TV shows portrays a funny lie. The world clearly says that lying is the way to go...but the Bible tells where.

Tell about a lie you or someone told as a child and consequences of it.

_____

_____

_____

_____

Deceit is not just a sin of modern times. The first lie was told by the father of lies, the devil, to Eve. She believed the lie and led the world into sin and death, influencing her husband Adam to join her in rebellion against God. From those parents came a murdering son, Cain, who lied directly to God pretending not to know what happened to Abel. People who are in rebellion always lie to the opponent. Isaac was deceived by Jacob who pretended to be Esau. Jacobs's sons showed him a bloody tunic, leading him to believe that his beloved son, Joseph, was savagely killed by wild animals, but Joseph had actually been sold into slavery. Pharaoh said the Israelites could leave Egypt nine times but reneged on the promise each time the plague was removed. Jezebel wrote letters in her husband's name and hired liars to witness against Naboth in order to have him stoned to death and acquire his vineyard for her selfish husband. The practice began with the first people and has continued throughout the ages.

Old Testament Precedent

Please read these verses and jot down a key phrase you find relevant and discuss.

Lev. 19:11-12_____

Ex. 18:21-22_____

Deut. 32:4_____

2 Kings 20:19_____

Ps. 86:11_____

Ex. 20:16_____

Ps. 119:104_____

Prov. 6:19_____

Prov. 17:4_____

Prov. 12:19-20_____

Prov. 12:22_____

James 5:12 But above all, my brethren, do not swear, either by heaven or by earth or with any other oath. But let your "Yes," be "Yes," and your "No," "No," lest you fall into judgment. NKJV This explains clearly that we should be so honest that swearing would not be necessary. If we say it, everyone, at least those who know us, should know that it is the truth. Trust between husband and wife is essential for a stable home. Often women tell with no shame that they were dishonest about their shopping practices, but nowhere in the Bible does it state that it is OK to deceive a stingy husband. Deceit about insignificant things destroys trust and can lead to lying about important things. *Gal 6:7-8* tells us that we can expect to be deceived if we deceive. Untold misery is caused by a dishonest partner.

Parents of deceitful teenagers must worry, always uncertain of where they are or what they are doing when they are out of sight. Children find it hard to understand that cheating in school robs the cheater of knowledge, but training in honesty will help them avoid many temptations.

New Testament Admonition

Please read these verses and jot down a key phrase you find relevant and discuss.

1 Tim. 1:10-11_____

Titus 1:10-11_____

Rev. 21:8_____

Rom. 16:17-18_____

Matt. 24:11-12_____

Eph. 5:9_____

Eph. 4:29_____

Mark 7:21-23_____

Col. 2:8_____

Rev. 14:5_____

Phil. 4:8_____

When Jesus was just a baby, Herod lied to the wise men who inquired about the new king saying that he wanted to worship him also. Liars with testimonies that did not agree testified against Jesus when he was brought before the high priests and council, yet He was condemned. It is astonishing that Jesus took the guilt of those liars along with our guilt when He hung on the cross.

Ananias, followed by Sapphira, suffered death after Peter inquired why had Satan filled his heart to lie to the Holy Spirit. God had allowed Ananias to profit from the sale of land and allowed him to choose to give or keep part of it, but the lie he told about it was not ignored. If Satan can tempt us to pretend to be "good", in this case generous, when we are another, God knows the truth even if our acquaintances do not.

As painful as it is to explain to a child that the world can be dangerous, everyone, especially children, must be warned of deceivers. Kidnappers and child molesters persuade children away from safety with a lie. Many young ladies have lost their virginity after believing the lie, "I love you and we'll get married." Robbing older people by scams is a growing problem in our country. In a perfect world we would not have to guard against dishonest people who will steal our identity and use our good credit to continue to steal, but sin in this world is rampant. Therefore, children must be taught to be trustworthy, yet aware that many in this world are not.

What lie have you believed and found out later it was false?

_____

_____

_____

_____

What if the lady who reached out and touched the robe of Jesus had said, "No, it wasn't me"? What if the little boy had said, "No, I didn't bring any fish"? What if Zacchaeus had said, "I want to be your disciple, Lord, but I never did cheat anybody"?

Reading the Bible with honest hearts leads us to the truth and sets us free from sin, according to the words of Jesus. *John 8:32* Have you ever been awakened from a bad dream and felt the tremendous joy of finding the truth? Perhaps heaven will be like that, the joy of awaking from the sorrows of the earth to the ecstasy of heaven.

I, _____ , will teach _____ to be truthful and warn of the dangers of believing a lie and practicing dishonesty.

Describe how you will teach a child to be honest.

_____

_____

Write It On Your Heart ♥ Memory verse: *John 3:21*
But he who does the truth comes to the light, that his deeds may be clearly seen, that they have been done in God." NKJV

Mama's granddaughter, Kelly Buchanan, says, "In my family, we say 'Liars are fryers!' because *Rev. 21:8* says *all liars will be cast into the lake of fire* and fear is a great motivator!"

Take It To Heart ♥ Fictional Dilemma for Don't Tell Stories

It was an honest mistake. Or was it? She really didn't look at the paper on purpose, it just was there. Marti had helped the teacher grade the papers from class A, which was part of her duty as teacher helper, and the test she was going to have in class B would be different, so no problem there. The teacher had told her to sit at the teacher's desk to work while she took a little break and Marti had done exactly that. When she reached inside a drawer, just to get a Kleenex, she couldn't help but see the test for class B right on top. She only looked for a minute, but it only took a minute to know that she needed to learn the very item she had not reviewed thoroughly. Fortunately, there was just enough time to learn it before the class period when she would take the test.

So the test grade was posted and Marti's grade was first. She made the best grade in class! Uuuuuh, the others had not seen the test before taking it...so was she cheating? Should she tell? Would the teacher ever trust her again?

Write From Your Heart ♥ Memory of *honesty is the best policy* incident

_____

_____

_____

_____

_____

_____

_____

_____

_____

_____

Mama's Cooking With Heart ♥
More Potatoes

Creamed Potatoes: Peel and cut into uniform pieces. Place in water and boil until tender. Drain off all the water. Use a hand mixer to bash them all to pieces. Add salt and butter and bash them again. Pour in milk or cream and mix again. When you have added enough milk for them to be in soft pillow mounds, your potatoes are ready to serve. Make plenty as the kids will want seconds.

Stewed Potatoes: Peel and boil as for mashed potatoes with small amount of salt and bacon grease. While they boil, mix a small handful of flour with water. When the potatoes are soft, add the flour mixture and boil a bit until the liquid thickens. Add pepper if you like. Serve to your meat and potatoes men.

Potato Salad: Peel and boil potatoes as usual with salt. When potatoes are tender, remove all the excess water and allow to cool. Cut into small bite size pieces. Add a few chopped boiled eggs, chopped sweet pickles, one chopped medium onion and a enough mayonnaise with a little bit of yellow mustard to coat every piece of potato. Taste it and add more salt if needed. Cool a good while and the grown-ups will like it.

MAMA SAID SAY YOUR PRAYER

Family Heartstrums ♥

After church on Sunday, Mama took the biscuits out of the oven, stacked up the fried chicken, dished up the gravy, called the grownups to the first table, and asked Uncle Buddy or Granddaddy to say the prayer before anyone could stick a fork into a pulley-bone. Waiting for our turn, sniffing the food and hoping there would be some good chicken parts left since Mama had fried two chickens, we kids tried to listen to the kin talk and tease with our stomachs growling. Finally the words, "Come on, Kids," and it was our turn to sit at the table and cover our biscuits with gravy, pick up a chicken leg or pulley-bone, spoon out a mound of creamed potatoes, and finish off with a slice of Mama's white cake with chocolate icing. Then it was off to the creek to swim, out to the basketball goal, or a game of softball in the yard, Daddy included. Occasionally, with only immediate family present, Mama prayed before supper.

Granddaddy's prayer at the table rose from his own heart, yet part of it became so familiar to his grandchildren we still recite it when we reminisce: "the food we are about to receive". As my brothers grew up they were included in the group of prayer leaders.

Although Mama's private prayers were offered during her time of solitude or at night before she slept, we were aware that she prayed. She prayed ceaselessly about us, about herself, about Daddy, about her family of origin, about the rulers of the land, etc. "OK, now, say your prayer" Mama reminded us as Mark, Tommy and I crawled into bed when we were little folks, just as she had reminded Bibbie, Dick, and Jack. "Now I lay me down to sleep" we recited until it became a part of our bedtime ritual. Growing in knowledge and faith, we then used that memorized prayer as a springboard to our personal thoughts.

Heart of the Matter ♥

In any mother's life, there are constantly reasons to pray in thanksgiving, praise, and to call for His help. In former times the Lord's prayer on a chart was posted in classrooms for public school students to read and repeat until it was known by heart. Those who attended Sunday Bible school or listened regularly to a preacher probably have learned David's famous prayer beginning, "Let the words of my mouth…." These memorized prayers can still be a part of our own individual prayers. Of course, if we use the Lord's model prayer, we must revise the "Thy kingdom come" line to an expression of thanks that His kingdom *has* come. Children who have been taught by their parents to speak personal things to God often touch our hearts and bring our smiles when one asks for a baby sister, when a two year old asks for a golf cart like his granddaddy's, or the older ones pray that the homeless will get a home.

Prayer is communication with God, essential for every occasion and circumstance of our life. When we are happy, then we should be praising, rejoicing that we are blessed by God's goodness, remembering that He is love and the source of all happiness.

James 1:17 Every good gift and every perfect gift is from above, and comes down from the Father of lights, with whom there is no variation or shadow of turning. NKJV

If we have troubles we must pray for his guidance and soak up the comfort with thankfulness. If we are tempted we must pray for his strength and wisdom and get in the Book for direction. A wonderful comfort comes from knowing that others are praying for us. It matters not a whit that prayers are outlawed at school except for the children who don't hear prayers at home: a praying person will pray anyway. Prayer doesn't have to be aloud. As the population of our country becomes more and more diverse, the public school teachers are also becoming more diverse in their philosophies. It is so much better to teach our children to pray silently than to have them endure a teacher leading a chant to an idol as the Buddhists do, or to Mary, or to Mohammed. Our teaching of prayer must be done at home and in Christian gathering places.

In times of stress and emergency, prayers may be all we can do, and is actually the most powerful thing one can do. We can find comfort by calling on fellow Christians to pray and having the assurance that an army of prayerful people were going before God on behalf of anyone in danger. Missionaries plead for prayers knowing that He is the source of their courage and Christians are the vital back-up force.

Think of a prayer you learned as a child and thank the person who taught you.

_____

_____

   To hear a prayer of praise and gratitude, listen to David's psalms; to hear a grieving lament for sin, listen to David's psalms; to hear a request for help, again, listen to David's psalms. Many women identify with Hannah who desperately prayed for a child and God gave her a son who grew up to be the prophet Samuel. From Isaac's prayer for a child from Rebekah, we may learn to be careful what we ask for, as he was given *twins who jostled with each other* even before they were born. God always responded to the cries of His people and sent them help when they turned to Him, as in the case of Moses, Gideon, and Nehemiah. Daniel, Shadrach, Meshach, and Abednego valued their privilege of prayer to Jehovah God to the extent that a lion's roar or a flaming fire did not stop them.

Old Testament Precedent

   Please read these verses and jot down a key phrase you find relevant and discuss.

Gen. 32:11_____

Ex. 8:8, 9;28_____

1 Kings 8:22,23,26,54_____

Ezra 6:10_____

Ps. 5:2_____

Ps. 69:13_____

Ps. 122:6_____

Jer. 29:12-13_____

Why should we pray? In order to talk to the Being in control! Citizens go to all kinds of trouble and expense to get to speak to the president, or the CEO of the company, to someone in charge of action. But we have instant access to the *real Power* who will always listen and respond in our best interest. First we should pray to acknowledge that He is God, that He is all powerful, all knowing, forever present, and all good. We should pray to acknowledge that He is light, love, hope, life and our Father. According to Paul we would receive even more blessings if we would just ask. *Eph 3:20 Now to Him who is able to do exceedingly abundantly above all that we ask or think, according to the power that works in us…NKJV* All wisdom or worthwhile knowledge is from Him. He is the source of our salvation; we can never, ever save ourselves.

New Testament Admonition
Please read these verses and jot down a key phrase you find relevant and discuss.

Matt. 5:44_____

Matt. 6:5-8_____

Matt. 6:9_____

Matt. 26:41_____

John 17:20-21_____

Rom. 8:26-27_____

1 Cor. 14:15_____

Col. 1:3-4_____

Col. 4:2-3_____

1 Thess. 5:16-18_____

James 5:13_____

3 John 2-3 _____

Jude 20_____

Jesus prayed for His followers to have unity with one another as He was unified with God. His apostles asked to be taught to pray so Jesus taught them a model prayer which included honoring the Father, acknowledgment of His will, thankfulness, and requesting forgiveness of sin. He also prayed when he dreaded the awful cross and the guilt of our darkest sins, but despite the sorrow, He prayed for God's will to prevail.

Our prayer should always address God in a way that acknowledges his Deity and gives Him praise. When the answer to a prayer request is not yes, our subsequent prayers should still be *Thank you God*, because if we truly prayed that His will be done, then He will overrule any request we make that is not in our best interest. God knows what we need and the Holy Spirit will make "intercession for the saints according to the will of God." *Rom 8:27* Isn't it comforting to know that, like a good parent, God will not be swayed by our pleading for something that would not be good for us? Realizing that God allowed His Son to suffer and recognizing the anguish from the words spoken to God from the cross helps us accept that suffering may be for a good purpose. Even though one may not identify the benefit of suffering or why our request is not met, faith and obedience will keep us thankful. Paul acknowledged that God did not take away his thorn in the flesh so God will not alleviate *all* our suffering, but He will help us bear it. The pain free, trouble free life is the next one, *the spiritual one*, not this earthly one.

Some prayers are a waste of time. *James 4:3* tells us that if we ask selfishly God will not honor it. A Pharisee who stood and bragged to God of his goodness went away unjustified. An unrighteous person with no desire to change has no avenue to God. The prayer that is prayed to impress men will do just that, impress men but not God. The Pharisees were show-offs with loud and long prayers, but Jesus told His disciples to pray in secret and God will reward them openly. When Balaam didn't want to hear God's advice and nagged Him for permission to go on a sinful mission, God sent him a talking donkey. Prayers about the destination of a deceased person will have no effect as seen in *Luke 16* when the unkind rich man pleaded with God to send a messenger back to earth to warn his brothers of torment. Prayers that are not sincere are vain babbling.

God has promised to reward those who diligently seek Him, as Cornelius was after he had offered prayers and gifts to the poor. Prayers seeking Him along with searching the scripture and allowing our minds to absorb truth will lead us on a walk in the light.

Remember a request that you made to God that in hindsight you know would not have been good for you.

_____

_____

Name five specific reasons you will praise God.

1._____

2._____

3._____

4._____

5._____

Children learn by mimicking what they see and hear. One good way to teach a child to pray is by saying a phrase and having the young one repeat it. Such as,

Adult: Dear Father in heaven   **Child**: Dear Father in heaven
Adult: Thank you for loving me **Child:** Thank you for loving me

What will you model for a child to say in prayer?

_____

_____

_____

_____

Write It On Your Heart ♥ _Memory verse: Ps 4:1 Hear me when I call, O God of my righteousness! You have relieved me in my distress; Have mercy on me, and hear my prayer. NKJV_

♥ Mama's granddaughter, Susan Pedersen, says, "Prayers are not about always having a 'yes' answer. God knows what is best for us and when it seems He is saying a simple big 'NO!' He is really saying He has something better in mind for us."

Take It To Heart ♥ Fictional Dilemma for Say Your Prayer

The list was about the same: her kids, their problems, her husband, somebody who was sick, ask for forgiveness, thanks for good day. ZZZZZZ Sleep overtook Cammie before she got halfway. Surely God wanted to hear from her at the end of the day and she had said _"thank you"_ a few times throughout the day but her main prayer was usually at night when things were shutting down. Oh, yeah, she was shutting down too.

Just today, when Harry wrecked his bike and knocked loose a tooth, she had prayed fervently, "Please, help, Dear God. Let him be OK" and when the dentist reported that it should tighten back up she whispered, "Thank you, God." And again, when she got so aggravated at Arri when he continued to delay his homework until she threatened mightily, she begged, "Dear God, please forgive me if I am impatient. Help me choose the right words tomorrow." So every day, it was a leaning on Him, and thanking Him, but the nighttime final prayer was getting short shift.

Cammie worried that God expected more from her, more praise and thankfulness, and more concern for unfortunate people who needed God. She tried, after kissing her husband good night, to turn her mind to Him, and for a moment she did, but if she didn't drift into sleep then thoughts of her kids slipped into her mind, or thoughts of the next day, or the upcoming family gathering, or if Arnold had a clean shirt ironed, or…

How can she control those thoughts and concentrate on a prayer God wanted from her? In fact, how can she ever cover all the points that need prayer?

Write From the Heart ♥ Memory of when you desperately prayed for God's help

_____

_____

_____

_____

_____

_____

_____

_____

_____

_____

_____

_____

_____

_____

Mama's Cooking With Heart ♥
Pinto Beans

Open a bag of dried pinto beans into a pot of water. Wash and pick out any tiny rocks that are sometimes lurking. Soak overnight.

The next morning, pour off the soaking water and add new, at least double the amount of beans, perhaps, 8 cups of water to 4 cups of beans that have swollen from their soak. Add a 2 inch by 1 inch chunk of pork fat back sliced almost but not quite apart. Bring to boil and continue to cook over a low heat for several hours. Serve with green onions in the spring, fresh tomatoes in the summer, and sweet bulb onions in fall and winter. And cornbread of course!

Cornbread

Buy a sack of Martha White Self-Rising cornmeal and follow the directions on the sack.

Bake in an iron skillet, a baking pan, muffin tins, or corn stick molds. Good with beans of *any* sort or with just a glass of milk.

Hoe Cake

Make the corn bread batter. Melt some bacon fat in a very hot iron skillet. Drop spoons of batter separately into the grease. Make them thicker than a pancake but as large as you want in diameter. Fill your skillet but one cake should not touch the another for a crispy edge. Watch closely. When the top bubbles and the edge turns brown, use an egg turner to peek under. When the cake is adequately brown, flip over and wait for the other side to brown. Take those out and do it all over again until you have enough to fill up your hungry brothers. Yummy with fresh green beans from the garden.

MAMA SAID DON'T BE SILLY

Family Heartstrums ♥

At last Daddy pulled into the gas station in Lebanon ... Yeaaaaa...halfway to Red Boiling Springs...but right now, we'd get an ice cream sandwich. This rare special treat was part of our trip routine on the three hour drive to see Daddy's folks. With the windows rolled down to get some relief from the heat, we watch the hills grow higher and the valleys deeper. Along one stretch of road we read the signs urging us to "See Rock City" or use Burma Shaving Cream. The fun part was not the reading of it; it was the changing of it that brought our laughter.

Try omitting the beginning sound of each word and substituting a B. "A penny saved is a penny earned" becomes "A benny baved bis a benny bearned" ....hilarious to a kid's mind. We would repeat such a sentence over and over trying different initial sounds. Silliness can be harmless as child's play or performed for entertainment. Normally we searched the newspapers to see what silly thing Dennis the Menace had done or how dumb the characters in

Lil Abner could be, happily glad we were smarter. The antics of the three stooges on television delighted us with their extreme silliness.

But all silliness is not harmless. Sometimes young girls can act pretty silly, giggling incessantly, whispering or talking too loudly and drawing undue attention. "Boy crazy" might be considered a synonym with silly. That's what Mama meant when she told me, "Don't be silly", not wanting to be embarrassed in church services or any other public place. She wanted me to be a lady and show a little sense. The warning was to prevent drawing an inordinate amount of attention to oneself by ridiculous behavior. Jesus taught, Matt 12:36 But I say to you that for every idle word men may speak, they will give account of it in the day of judgment. NKJV

Heart of the Matter ♥

In the Bible foolish is a synonym with silly. You probably remember a fairy tale or two about the three sillies of one sort or another who somehow managed to outwit the powerful. Regardless of that bit of fun, the Bible does not lead us to believe anything good will come out of foolish thoughts or actions; in fact, we are warned many times of the reverse. Silly or foolish actions bring devastating results.

Fools do not use their brains for learning or reasoning but simply act without regard for the consequences. Samson was the strong man, but how foolish he was to believe Delilah. Why didn't he know he could not trust her when each time he told her a false source of his strength, she tried to disable him? Surely he should know she would try it when he told her the truth. She was the enemy; she was a liar; she was not a worshipper of God, but he confided in her. Shame on Samson. Shame on us if we trust dishonest people who blatantly serve the devil. God used Samson in spite of his silly ways, but Samson had to suffer the consequences and serve in a way that took his own life.

Remember a time when you were in a situation so hilarious you could not stop laughing but now the same situation does not seem funny.

_____

_____

_____

_____

_____

Moses, coming down Mt. Sinai carrying the two tablets of stone engraved by the finger of God, looked down upon a spectacle of fools. The Hebrew people who had witnessed the plagues against Egypt and the parting of the Red Sea were dancing around a golden calf, forgetting the all powerful Jehovah who brought them out of slavery, to bow before a mute, deaf, paralyzed, dumb statue. They forgot their struggles and began to have fun. *Exodus. 32:5 ... Aaron saw [this], he built an altar before it..... 6. So the next day they rose early and offered burnt offerings, and brought peace offerings; and the people sat down to eat and to drink, and rose up to play.* Listen to the foolish explanation Aaron gave, *Exodus 32:24 And I said to them, 'Whoever has any gold, let them break it off.' So they gave it to me, and I cast it into the fire, and this calf came out." NKJV*

So exasperated as not to think clearly, Moses threw down the tablets, breaking them. What a wonderful, merciful God we have who wrote the commandments on stone again with His own hand! Thankfully, Moses prayed and God did not destroy these foolish people but devised a plan to save them. The useless golden statue was crushed and put into their drinking water. You'd think we would learn!

Old Testament Precedent
Please read these verses and jot down a key phrase you find relevant and discuss.

Prov. 9:13_____

Prov. 10:14_____

Prov. 10:21_____

Prov. 14:9_____

Prov. 15:2_____

Prov. 15:14_____

Prov. 15:21_____

Prov. 18:6-7_____

Prov. 20:15_____

Eccl. 10:11-14_____

Eccl. 7:17_____

Jesus spoke of silly girls as opposed to sensible ones in the parable of the foolish virgins in *Matt 25:1-25*. Can you imagine what the foolish virgins might have said when they returned home? "Mama, why didn't you make me take more oil? You knew my lamp was almost empty! What? How was I to know it would get that dark? My lamp had some oil in it; I thought that would be enough. There was something wrong with my lamp; it used my oil up too fast! That oil must have been inferior; it burned up too fast! But, Mama, I didn't have time; Roseate was waiting for me already. I didn't hear you say anything about taking any extra oil, besides I might have spilled oil on my new robe! Who wanted to go to that old wedding anyway? So? My friends didn't get to go either... only those with nothing better to do than fill lamps! Oh, Mama, why does nobody like me? They let those other girls in but I never get to do anything. Can you believe they actually locked the gate? He shouldn't have made us wait so long! He said he didn't know us, but he was talking to us just yesterday! But in their hearts, they must have said, "I could have been with the bridegroom but I was not prepared."

What silly excuse have you made when you were unprepared for something?

_____

_____

_____

_____

New Testament Admonition
Please read these verses and jot down a key phrase you find relevant and discuss.

Matt. 5:22 _____

1 Pet. 1:13_____

2 Tim. 2:23_____

2 Tim. 3:6_____

Titus 1:10 _____

Titus 2:11-12_____

Titus 3:9 _____

Girls do not have a patent on silliness. Look at the parable of the foolish man who built his house on sand. *Matthew 7* How foolish can one get? Sure, sand is easy to move and level. Yes, it will move right out from under the house! Rock has to be chipped away bit by bit. Can you imagine trying to fasten something to a rock? Who wants to do that? Only someone who needs something to last forever; only someone who believes in doing a thing the right way the first time; only someone who knows the importance of a foundation; only someone who thinks and has an awareness of consequences. If we can teach children to reason, to think of consequences of behavior, then they will be on the narrow path that leads to a permanent home. The blessing of choice, of free will, is given to us along with promises of reward and warnings of punishment. We are told in advance so we have no excuse!

We have no excuse, but we do have a merciful Father! Not one of us has avoided all foolish mistakes either by thoughtlessness or purposefully. Wonderful indeed it is that Jesus made a plan for us to be forgiven of our foolishness if we are truly sorry and follow His plan of repentance and forgiveness.

Think of a time that you were foolish and would behave in a different way if you had known then what you know now.

_____

_____

_____

Teach someone this reasoning. 1. God rewards those who obey. 2. I want a reward. 3. Therefore I will _____ _____.

The rich fool thought that he had made the right decisions by planting and harvesting a bumper crop. He was so confident that he thought, "I'm such a good farmer! I must build bigger barns!" But God thought differently. A fool is *Luke 12:21 ... he who lays up treasure for himself, and is not rich toward God."* His soul was required elsewhere and he could not haul a single sack of grain with him. The farmer's methods of agriculture must have been exemplary, but his use of his blessings was deplorable. Did he actually own the rain and soil or just use them?

As a sojourner in a transient land one must know value and teach our children to discern the difference between authentic, everlasting treasure and temporary, worldly, imitation blessings. It is a comfort to know that everlasting treasure can be stored, but not here. *Matt 19:21 Jesus said to him, "If you want to be perfect, go, sell what you have and give to the poor, and you will have treasure in heaven; and come, follow Me." 2 Cor. 4:18 For the things which are seen are temporary, but the things which are not seen are eternal. NKJV*

God gave us Jesus to be a perfect sacrifice but also as a perfect example and teacher. The parables found in the gospels give us the same information that the apostles were given. The other books expand on the teachings as the writers were given inspiration by the Holy Spirit. James teaches us to have patience, to wait for the ultimate reward rather than seeking fleeting temporary pleasures. Wisdom brings joy and peace on earth because we can know we are saved, but we have the promise of indescribable bliss in eternity when our treasure chest of everlasting jewels will be opened. Silliness is a temporary, momentary shallow hilarity, but eternal happiness is found through a reasoning faith.

I, _____, will teach _____to store these treasures in heaven. 1_____ 2_____

How will you do this? _____

Write It On Your Heart ♥ Memory verse: *Prov. 21:20 There is desirable treasure, oil in the dwelling of the wise, But a foolish man squanders it. NKJV*

Mama's granddaughter, Sandy Faires says, "Others need to see Christ in us, radiating a faith and a joy that is pure and genuine. But sadly that can be overshadowed by our foolish words or behavior. May we have the courage to learn His ways and walk in wisdom, shining brightly in this dark world."

Take it to Heart ♥ Fictional Dilemma for Don't Be Silly

"Wow!" the sales clerk exclaimed. "Those jeans were made for you!" Abbey agreed that the jeans fit perfectly, just the exact look she had hoped to find. Turning this way and that to get a full view in the three mirrors, she was pleased to note the ten pounds she had lost left her looking good. Her short legs actually looked longer and slimmer and with the new boots in the shop around the corner she would look even better. *Matt will sit up and take notice now,* she thought. *He'll be so proud of me at the company picnic.* But the next thought came uninvited, *No, he won't be proud, he'll be angry.*

A few days had passed since they paid the bills and the worry had eased up a little. They had made the minimum payment on all the credit cards and she had promised she would not charge a thing this month. Dave Ramsey had done a number on Matt. He actually believes they can pay down the debt and build wealth if they just won't add any more debt. But where's the fun in scrounging? She would be the only wife there who hadn't spent a dime this week on clothes or jewelry! Recently the TV talk show she watched had demonstrated how to buy the best pair of jeans for each body type and these are exactly right for hers.

Setting financial goals had sounded sensible when they had worked out the plan and seeing it on paper gave her hope of buying a house next year and then having a baby. Matt even talked about planning for retirement a zillion years away. But it surely wouldn't hurt for one little outfit to go on the card. Or maybe they could just cut back their giving this once time. Jesus didn't say exactly how much "as you have been prospered" meant.

She knew the plan, but she has to have a decent self-image and Matt likes for her to look nice. And doesn't she deserve a reward for losing that ten pounds? Her other jeans are actually a bit loose now and these are just right. After she gets pregnant, jeans like this will be out of the question. But they aren't free. She knew her Macy's card wasn't maxxed out since they sent in the last payment so ....She knew about the rich man who was called a fool for wanting more and more but this was not like that was it?

Write From the Heart ♥ Memory of a silly event or foolish decision.

_____

_____

_____

_____

_____

_____

_____

_____

Mama's Cooking With Heart ♥

Coffee Hog

Pour a cup of coffee, not quite full, add milk and pieces of biscuit. Enjoy the warm comfort.☺

Molasses

Daddy and sons plant crop of cane sorghum. When it is so tall, cut the cane with a machete or ax and stack in heaps. Get Granddaddy to come help. Strip the leaves from each cane. Press the cane through a mill to squeeze out the juice into vats. Urge the horse to keep on going around, pulling the log lever in a slow circle. Give a 3 inch piece of sweet cane to each child. Teach kids how to peel and chew to get the sweet juice. Build a fire under the flat rectangular vats and cook the juice, forcing it to move from one vat to the next as it thickens. When the juice is reduced to a rich brown syrup, it is molasses, ready for a hot buttered biscuit. Store in Mason jars.

Mama's Great-granddaughters Cook ♥ with Heart and Convenience

Salad by Kat Fortner

First you slice some lettuce up in a bowl. Next you get some tomato and add it in with the lettuce in a bowl. Then you add croutons in the bowl. Last you add Ranch and you're done.

MAMA SAID KEEP YOURSELF PURE

Family Heartstrums ♥

Daddy and the boys milked the cows early one September day so we could go to the fair! "I want to ride the Tilt-a-Whirl," Mark and I both begged. Mama held on to little Tommy and only let him ride in a little car going round and round in circles. That Ferris Wheel was so far up that it hurt my neck to look that high to search for Bibbie, Dick, or Jack swinging in those little seats with their friends. Fun, fun, fun was the carnival, but there was one area where we were not to stop; that one where the girls stood out on a little stage and "hoochi cooched," enticing the men to come on in. Maybe my brothers sneaked in but if they did they sure didn't tell it at home.

"Don't have sex before you are married." Did Mama say that? Nope, I don't think so.....the word 'sex' was taboo. Actually I thought it would kill Mama or shame her to the vegetative state if I got pregnant out of wedlock. Adult ladies didn't talk openly about sex, but sixth-graders sure did. We reported things we overheard and things older friends told us. Somehow the message got *around. If one of my classmates knew, then the rest of us would soon know. Sex was for marriage and any behavior that might lead to impure activity should also be avoided. There was a noticeable difference in sentiment when Mama heard that someone was getting married by choice than when someone had to get married; the lightness of joy compared to a tone of grief.*

Heart of the Matter ♥

Until the late 1900's, premarital sex was considered to be the darkest of sin, yet it was practiced by some, especially by boys. In the *boys will be boys* double standard of that time, the same sin that was a shame for girls was overlooked by society in boys who committed fornication with *certain* girls. Homosexuality existed from olden times, as we know of Sodom and Gomorrah but until the present generation it was considered too awful to discuss. The Old Testament reveals that sexual sin was prevalent even though God assigned severe punishment for those practicing such. Accurate information is not always available for the young; therefore, many false things are believed.

Remember something funny you may have believed before you learned the truth of sex or having babies.

_____

_____

_____

_____

_____

_____

Although sin is not grouped by God into light sin and dark sin, the consequences of premarital and extramarital sex extend far beyond the couple. At least two families and their close friends are involved emotionally and spiritually. Parents may be angry, ashamed, disappointed, confused, and convicted of their own failure to teach. Close friends may be surprised and disappointed or may feel, as a peer, that they too should go ahead and participate. Shame may be a thing of the past according to the media, but this is not always true in reality. As the Bible teaches, the time has come when good is called evil and evil is called good. But the world's label does not make truth.

Tell about a fun experience you and your friends had during your dating years.

_____

_____

_____

_____

_____

Sexual sin brings heartbreaking decisions and plans for the future are *always* altered. If the consequence of the sin brings a beloved child, there still are inevitable difficulties. Who will support the child and how? Who will be the primary care giver? Who will assist in the care? The support and nurture of a child is not a one-person job. Someday, someone will have to explain to the child how his birth affected the family. Will the couple marry sooner without adequate financial capabilities? Will the education of the couple be terminated? Will the child be given to an adoptive family? Will the child be aborted? How will others, who have looked at the participants as role models, be persuaded that this sinful activity should not, *must not,* be imitated? Often all these difficult questions must be answered by teens whose brains are not fully adult.

Even when the consequence of premarital sex is not a pregnancy, the fact of lost virginity and the sin of immorality still brings an altered future because the sin is known to God, the participants and their future mates. Once sexual appetite is awakened, it must be dealt with, either by suppression or expression. The experience, although forgiven in the case of Christians who truly repent, is always remembered and regretted. If non-Christians fail to experience regret and seek forgiveness, then the tragedy is even greater.

2 Corinthians 7:10 *For godly sorrow produces repentance leading to salvation, not to be regretted; but the sorrow of the world produces death. NKJV*

Keeping pure and marrying someone who is also sexually pure brings many blessings. If both have reserved this special expression of love and intimacy for their spouse only, then it is a double gift. Sexual pleasure that God planned for husband and wife exclusively adds to the bond of love through activities shared by no other.

The gift of good health is invaluable with many diseases avoided completely and the risk of contracting many other diseases greatly diminished. Hopefully, everyone is aware of AIDS, genital herpes, gonorrhea, and genital warts. If not, go to the Internet and type in sexually transmitted diseases or find books in the library and get the facts you will need to teach your young people.

The Old Testament records many examples of individuals who were drawn into sexual sin. Samson's strength was sapped after Delilah enticed him and snipped his locks. David's sin of adultery with Bathsheba led to the deception and murder of her husband, Uriah, and consequently the death of their first baby son. Read in Psalms of David's anguish following this sin against God.

Some countries today assign the same punishment for a woman caught in adultery as God assigned during the Mosaical Period. For God to assign such a dire consequence suggests strongly that the family unit is a critical component for the care and training of children. **If the family is destroyed, then the makeup of human society is distorted.** Enigmatically, some of the countries who have severe laws concerning women also allow men to have multiple wives. Because the first laws of the United States were influenced by Christianity, the blessing of Christ is immeasurable in life even here on earth.

What right do you as a woman enjoy because the laws of the United States were based somewhat on Bible standards?

_____

_____

_____

Old Testament Precedent

Please read these verses and jot down a key phrase you find relevant and discuss.

Lev. 18:20 _____

Isa. 62:5 _____

Ex. 22:16-17 _____

Lev. 21:13 _____

Prov. 6:24 _____

Pro. 7:21 _____

No one can say that God didn't make it plain. The Bible writers, inspired by God, were not timid about informing us of the rightness and wrongness of sexual acts. God placed sexual desire in man from the beginning for the purpose of procreation and for the mutual drawing together of man and woman as one unit. God provided Eve for Adam that he might have a partner like himself, yet different and complementary. To the Israelites, God gave the Ten Commandments followed by explicit commands for sexual behavior.

Even though you may be too embarrassed to speak it aloud in a public situation, think back and remember how you learned about sexuality and decide if it was taught to you correctly. Many mistaken ideas are passed from child to child, teenager to teenager, and even from adults. .

What is being taught by television to the entire world that is the opposite of what the Bible teaches?

_____

_____

_____

_____

_____

The temptation of sexual sin has always been present, but today our youth are being bombarded with nudity and enticements not mentioned publicly in past generations. Our young people can only be protected by the armor that Paul describes in *Eph.6: 13-18*. Just as any soldier is helpless without armor and weapons, so is mankind helpless without the protection which God has provided. Also, like a soldier, one must by trained and willing to use it and wear it. Warnings of illness without the Bible standard will not work when a teenager believes the media and admires those that participate in and promote sinful practices. A teenager is very unlikely to put on the armor unless he is trained as a child. We must help them become accustomed to the restraints and to trust in the promises of God's protection. Swinging the two-edged sword correctly takes training! That's our job as parents, grandparents, friends, and role models.

Tell a true romance story, either yours or another.

_____

_____

_____

_____

New Testament Admonition

Please read these verses and jot down a key phrase you find relevant and discuss.

Acts 15:20 _____

Rom. 1:28-30_____

1 Cor. 5:11_____

1 Cor. 6:13_____

1Cor. 6:18_____

1Cor. 7:2-3_____

Gal. 5:19_____

Eph.5:2-5_____

Col. 3:5_____

1 Thess. 4:3-5_____

Jude 7_____

Rev. 21:8_____

The world of today teaches our young that girls should aspire to be sexy, appealing to men. This encourages temptation not only for herself but also for the boys and men who see her. The world teaches her that she should tempt men, and women who do so are rewarded with wealth and honor in many cases. One young lady attempting to break into the music industry was told by a record company representative that every male in the audience should want to have sex with her. Is it any wonder that the world is a dangerous place for girls?

Statistics indicate that one out of three women has been sexually abused or molested in some way. Many abuses go unreported because victims are reluctant to relive the trauma caused by having to repeat the story so many times to authorities. Some women claim the right to seduce and then say *no,* but the Bible condemns such dangerous behavior. Pedophiles and predators are on the prowl, now even by Internet, and sin is portrayed as good by the media; therefore we must be aware, as never before, and our youth must be educated and guarded.

Jesus did not practice the double standard as we see by His treatment of the adulterous woman who was brought to Him. The men were challenged as being just as guilty and she was told to go forth and sin no more, not condemned and stoned.

Tell about your wedding or the wedding of your friend. What made it romantic? _____

_____

_____

How can we be an influence for purity in the lives of the children in our families and in our church family?

_____

_____

Commitment: I, _____, will by example and teaching God's word strive to influence _____ to lead a pure life.

Write It On Your Heart ♥ Memory verse: 1 *Tim 4:12 Let no one look down on your youthfulness, ... NASB*

♥   **Mama's granddaughter, Dana Johnson, says,** "As a mother of three teenagers as well as a teacher of pre-teens, my awareness of impurity has been heightened. God's command for purity is not only a requirement, but a protection for his people. The consequences (mentally and physically) of impurity are many and often life altering. Purity allows much joy and peace that can last a lifetime."

Take It To Heart ♥ Fictional Dilemma for Keep Pure

Janie could hardly believe that Carl had finally asked her out. The basketball court gave her a good hour of gazing; secretly admiring the rippling muscles of his strong, long arms and legs while pretending to be absorbed in the game and thrilled by the action. When his brown eyes fringed with long dark lashes fell on her and his lips curved into a smile right in front of her she could hardly answer but the high, weak "yes" squeaked out. What would her mother say? Did she know his reputation? Probably not. She didn't talk much to people he knew. Most of her talking was to relatives or church people. How would she know that he made out with plenty of those girls? Nah, she wouldn't know. They say he brings beer but surely he would not do that with her. Everybody knows she doesn't drink so he has to know that too. Janie knew she could give him just what he needed, *plenty of admiration,* and then she would persuade him to go to church with her and he would see that fornication was wrong and he would admire her for being virtuous and respect her and what?...Marry her?

Meanwhile, what would others say? Her friends knew what was usually on Carl's mind. His innuendos were not very veiled. Everyone knows he's handsome! and funny! and he asked her out! Where would they go? Actually she knew. The same place he took the other girls..... to the movie and then to a lonely road....no, can't do that...maybe they would just go get a Coke and walk through the park....or bowling...or just stay at her house and watch TV...no he would never do that. Maybe they would go get a pizza and come home and play a game. OK, just one time and see what he's like, maybe everyone is wrong, maybe he just needs the right girl. What would people say? Everyone knows what he usually does....will they think she's like all the other girls he's dated?

What would Jesus do? He ate with publicans and sinners, He came to save the lost, He came as a physician to the sick not the well. So He would befriend with Carl. But would Carl spend time with Jesus? Well at this point, probably not. Jesus also said to go into the world and preach the gospel. Was this an opportunity to teach Carl? Probably not. OK.... that's where we'll go....to the youth game night...Mother will approve of that....if he refuses then then what will I do? _____

_____

_____

_____

_____

_____

_____

_____

_____

_____

_____

Write It From the Heart ♥ Memory of Teen Girl Friend Gab Session

_____

_____

_____

_____

_____

_____

_____

_____

_____

_____

_____

_____

_____

_____

_____

_____

_____

_____

_____

_____

_____

_____

_____

_____

_____

_____

_____

_____

Mama's Cooking With Heart ♥
Strawberry Preserves

strawberries

sugar

Travel three hours to where good strawberries ripen in May. Go to the strawberry patch when it is still cool enough for a jacket and the plants are wet with dew.

Take a small wooden box, bend to the ground and fill the box with the red strawberries…not the whitish green. Repeat several times until your back is aching and your daddy says you may quit picking and he will continue. Travel home the same day before the strawberries lose any freshness.

Wash each berry and cut off the little green cap at the top. Place in a thick pot. Put as much sugar as berries (one to one cup ratio) with a tiny bit of water to get the steam going. Cook until the sugar is melted and the berries have cooked. Just taste it to see if it's good and stop cooking. Watch closely as that sugar can burn!

Serve right away on hot biscuits with melted butter or place in a Mason glass jar and seal the lid while it is still hot for use next winter.

Mama's Great-granddaughters Cook ♥ with Heart and Convenience

Sleepover Dip texted by Callie Johnson

U need these ingredients 8 oz cream cheese 16 oz sour cream Phil. regular spicy halapeno 2 pkg Ranch dip mix jar of diced halopenos 1 bunch cilantro blend til creamy n lumps r out—takes 4ever! blend n both pkgs Ranch mix..blend in halopenos..abt 3 spoons for mild…add more to burn..blend in cilantro. Chill…teens love with tortilla chips.

MAMA SAID MARRIAGE IS FOR LIFE

Family Heartstrums♥

We watched from a window across the porch in our L shaped house....trying not to be obvious...but we watched Earl Mack walk up to the door and knock on the screen door, (totally unnecessary because Bibbie had been watching for him) handsome in his Air Force uniform. We watched Bibbie open the door but we couldn't see the rest until they walked out with his hand on her shoulder. I soaked up the romance but her brothers would tease her unmercifully later about anything she did or said. One day, however, she dressed in a new dress, looking just perfect, and left for good, going to get married. Mama cried a little bit to see her first child going off with another couple for witnesses, an accepted custom of the day, to marry and leave us.

It's hard to imagine that marrying would bring such a change; Bibbie's room was available, no big sister to fix my hair, pies would be cut into seven pieces, but best of all, we got Earl Mack, forever. On the weekends when they returned to spend a couple of days, we rushed out *to greet them and Bibbie's room was turned back to them. Earl Mack just joined right in with my brothers hunting, teasing, and eating at Mama's table.*

One after another, we married our sweethearts, knowing the Bible had instructions about marriage. Drummed into our heads by Mama was, "When you marry, you marry for always. There is no changing your mind after you get into it." I joyfully accepted the "Whither thou goest, I will go", and moved off to Kentucky, but with every intention of keeping close touch with my family of origin.

Heart of the Matter ♥

Divorce had touched our lives when a close relative was divorced by one unhappy wife and later married another. There were no light jokes about this or other broken marriages; instead the difference in treatment of a son and stepson was sadly noted. Christians endeavor to teach the permanency of marriage in a world that views marriage as a temporary arrangement. We need to understand that marriage vows are promises and that Christians do not break promises. "Let not man put asunder" means unbreakable. Even though the government grants a divorce, God does *not,* except for sexual immorality committed by one of the marriage partners.

As a bit of insurance against the possibility of divorce, our youth should be encouraged to marry Christians, with the hope that Christian mates will both agree that pleasing God will be the driving force in their lives. When our young become interested in dating, the first question should not be "What does he/she look like?" It should be "Is he/she a Christian?"

When you married, what caused you to think it would last forever?

_____

_____

_____

_____

_____

Woman should never forget that she was made for the man because he needed her as a suitable helper as no other creature can be. The creation story shows clearly that man was created and given the role of leader, but he was in need of a woman. The fact that Eve influenced Adam to do wrong, even though he knew he was disobeying God, demonstrates that women have a tremendous influence on the decisions and actions of man.

God's plan was one wife for one man as long as they both live, yet many characters in Old Testament times did otherwise. Even though Sarah had suggested Abraham take her handmaid to bring a child into the family, jealousy reared its ugly head and led to atrocious behavior by both wives and to the driving out of Ishmael and his mother, Hagar *Gen. 16.* Think of the pain in the family of Jacob who favored Rachel and her children over the other family members. *Gen 30* Remember that Solomon, after a life of indulgence with many wives and concubines, declares that it was all foolishness. *Ecclesiastes 1* The Savior teaches us that a writ of divorce was given by Moses but it was not with God's approval. *Matt 19:8 He said to them, "Moses, because of the hardness of your hearts, permitted you to divorce your wives, but from the beginning it was not so. NKJV*

Old Testament Precedent

Please read these verses and jot down a key phrase you find relevant and discuss.

Gen. 2:24_____

Ex. 22:16_____

Lev. 20:10_____

Prov. 5:18_____

Prov. 18:22_____

Prov. 19:13-14_____

Eccl. 9:9_____

Song of Sol. 4_____

Common sense tells us that children deserve to live with and love both their parents. God's design was always to have both parents nurture their children. A mother can not be a father and a father can never be a mother. God made men and women, not to duplicate one another, but to complement each other. Different attributes contribute to a home by the male and female, usually with the mother being more nurturing with a strong homemaking instinct and the father giving leadership, providing finances, and protection. The guidance and training by both parents are necessary for providing the optimal advantages of a Godly home. Today's secular marriage experts are admitting that children benefit from parents that choose to stay together even if the marriage relationship is difficult. As always the best advice is Bible based, so families in crisis should seek Christian counselors to help them compromise and revise their behavior. This, of course, does not imply that children should be unsheltered in an abusive, dangerous home.

Same-sex partnerships, actually not a marriage, are completely sinful according to God's word and from common sense. This behavior, despite being commonly practiced and accepted by the world, is just one more of the anti-Christ practices being promoted by Satan. *1 Cor. 6:9* Children would not even be possible in such a relationship except by using extra-ordinary methods of conception or by adoption.

Relate when you recognized a trait in someone that would make a good husband.

_____

_____

_____

_____

_____

Write about one of your traits that make a good wife.

_____

_____

_____

_____

_____

New Testament Admonition

    Please read these verses and jot down a key phrase you find relevant and discuss.

Matt. 5:31-32_____

Matt. 19:19_____

Col. 3:18-19_____

1 Cor. 7:2-5_____

Hebrews 13:4_____

1 Cor. 7:10-11_____

1 Cor. 7:39_____

Eph. 5:23-25_____

Eph. 5:28_____

Eph. 5:33_____

1 Tim. 5:9_____

1 Peter 3:7_____

In our society children will be intermingling with persons involved in ungodly "marriages", cohabiting situations, families with children switched to and fro between two homes. **How can you explain to a child that God's way is the best?** _____

_____

_____

_____

Many families must deal with the broken heart of a child whose parents have broken his home and may feel unloved by or homesick for the absent parent. **How can you help that child feel the constant love of God?** _____

_____

_____

_____

For a child to learn what a good, happy marriage is, the model of such a marriage should be in his experience. Respect and love between the marriage partners is the best way for a child to learn and emulate, just as the best way for a child to learn to love God is to see his parents love God. If a child can not find this experience at home, then the church should provide such an experience. Teachers of our Bible classes and other caring adults who have a God inspired, happy environment should be willing to invite children to their home. Boys need to witness how a caring husband treats his wife, and girls need to observe that being in submission to a loving husband is a rewarding position. One of the sweetest pictures on earth is that of an older couple who have spent their lives loving one another. Seniors who have had such a life will be happy to relate wonderful memories that appeal to the romantic nature of our young people.

One older Christian lady credits the providence of God with helping her to recognize the man with the attributes she had already decided her husband must have. She remembers being fascinated by a young man who did not have such characteristics, but because her family moved away from that community, she was able to distinguish between infatuation and real love. Such couples are excellent role models for all the young people if their story is told.

We must teach our children to seek a partner with characteristics that will enhance a life long marriage. *Titus 2:4-5* teaches us that older women should, *"admonish the young women to love their husbands, to love their children, to be discreet, chaste, homemakers, good, obedient to their own husbands, that the word of God may not be blasphemed." NKJV*

Interview an older Christian couple you know and write a brief summary of their love story.

_____

_____

_____

_____

_____

_____

One of God's greatest earthly blessings is a faithful spouse who delights in the joy of the other. Couples with different interests and talents can each adapt and respect the interests of the other. The willingness to try the ideas of our spouse will likely enrich our lives with varied experiences. One who can't draw a straight line may delight in art by another or a non-athlete may become an avid fan of their sweetie on the field. We must all pray ceaselessly that God will bless our families with love for one another but as second place to their love for God. Even if a couple can not experience all things together, one can always respect and encourage the other. How difficult it must be for the spouse of one involved in extreme sports or costly hobbies. Each person must also be aware of the financial and emotional drain a selfish interest might be to the family. Some words of advice sound easy, but compromising about things we hold dear is very difficult. We need to call for God's help through prayer, give Him thanks for our marriage, and then live by His advice.

Commitment: I, _____, will teach _____ that God wants him/her to give and receive love and trust in a marriage that lasts throughout their life.
How will you do this ? _____

_____

_____

Write It On Your Heart ♥ Memory verse: *Proverbs 31:11 The heart of her husband safely trusts her; So he will have no lack of gain. NKJV*

♥ Mama's granddaughter, Sandy Faires says, "I never shared a conversation or a song with my grandmother, never even heard her voice since her time here ended before mine began. Still, I can hear my grandmother's words as family members share the truths she spoke and lived. And I can hear her words as I read my Bible because so much of what she spoke was God's word. Her life of faithfulness has blessed me in my life, in my marriage, and with my own children. She left a timeless spiritual legacy to me to pass down to my daughter and son, for which I am eternally grateful to God."

Take It To Heart ♥ Fictional Dilemma for Marriage Is For Life

"You're fired!" slammed the door to income, prestige, and honor, and dealt a blow to his healthy self-image. Joan could feel the pain when he told her of the traumatic situation and rushed to hug and comfort him. Their tears mingled at the unfairness of his treatment after years of loyalty to the company. Surely, the new management could easily review the past performance and see that Darrell had been a valuable performer, and that his wisdom would be more valuable than the new younger employee's idea spurts.

When the finality sank in, the questions began. Will unemployment be enough? No, it wouldn't, not if they continued to live in the same manner. Where would he find another job? She didn't want to move to Timbuktu! Would they have to move from their spacious house? Now would the kids be able to go to the Christian university or any university for that matter? Should she try to work more ....but what would happen to the kids after school? She pushed her anxiety into the background and said, "Darrell, God has always cared for us and He will not fail us now."

But months followed months with no job in sight. Anger set in, anger at her, though it wasn't her fault. Even when she took on overtime, he still attacked at every late meal, at every wrinkled shirt, at every time she was delayed getting home. Would it never stop? Maybe the marriage should stop....would he straighten up if she walked out? Maybe she should just show that Darrell he still had something to lose!

Write From Your Heart ♥ Memory of a loving married couple

_____

_____

_____

_____

_____

_____

_____

_____

_____

_____

_____

_____

_____

_____

_____

_____

_____

_____

_____

_____

_____

_____

_____

_____

_____

_____

Mama's Cooking With Heart ♥

Chocolate Pie

11/2 cups sugar	3 tbsp cocoa
1/3 cup flour	1 tbsp vanilla
2 cups milk infused with cream	½ stick butter
3 eggs separated	

Combine sugar, flour and cocoa in a heavy sauce pan. Mix in milk. Turn on high heat and beat the egg yolks slightly. Stir about ½ cup of the warm chocolate mixture into the egg yolks. Turn heat down to medium and stir egg mixture into the sauce pan mixture. Stir continuously scraping the bottom. Cook and stir until it becomes thick. Take off heat and stir in butter and vanilla.

Pour into a baked crust. Make meringue and place completely over custard. Bake at 350 degrees until light brown. Cool, cut into 8 even pieces, set aside until after dinner. Watch out for the one who likes to poke his finger in the biggest piece claiming it as his.

Mama's Great-granddaughters Cook ♥ with Heart and Convenience

Vanilla Pudding by Ella Faires

Open the vanilla box of pudding. Pour it in the bowl. Pour in 1 cup of milk. Wisk it for 1 minute. Put it in the refrigerator for 1 hour and Enjoy!

Write a letter to a someone and tell them what you hope for them concerning marriage.

_____

_____

_____

_____

_____

_____

_____

_____

_____

_____

_____

_____

_____

_____

_____

_____

_____

_____

_____

_____

_____

_____

_____

_____

_____

_____

MAMA SAID OBEY THE GOSPEL

Family Heartstrums ♥

"Now, Buddy, you know better than that!" Mama would argue when Uncle Buddy, playing devil's advocate, would spout that one only had to believe to be saved. And of course he did know better. "Peter said plainly in Acts 2:38 to believe and be baptized," she proved, but the debate would continue on that and other aspects of the gospel. Sunday afternoons often took such a turn at our house when Uncle Buddy, Aunt Mary, Patsy, and Jerry came for fried chicken and banana pudding..

Sometimes the sound of four-part harmony filled us with joy as they practiced for quartet singing at someone's funeral. Mama's alto voice was etched in our memory, as was a love for a cappella singing. Another friendly debate about instrumental music trained us to know that we honor God by worshipping Him as He said, without adding something that might please our ears. Mama could never take the devil's advocate part. Her conscience would never allow her to go against the Bible even in jest, thinking, "What if *someone heard only that part and believed it?"*

We kids did hear it, both sides, and believed the Bible. We believed what those preachers shouted out straight from Acts 2. "Repent and be baptized!"

Heart of the Matter ♥

In our summer time gospel meetings, while hand-held funeral home fans swished, the preachers declared with emphasis that any listener must choose between two final destinations possible for every human being *Rev. 21.* Christians go to heaven because they are forgiven. Others who refuse God's forgiveness go to hell. It's a choice. Our hearts drummed with excitement when sinners stood, confessed their faith that Jesus is the Son of God, proclaimed by their actions a repentance of sins, and were baptized into Christ. Women often cried, being filled with the emotion of someone obeying their Lord.

To be a Christian mother means raising children who have the facts. How can a child begin to make righteous decisions independently if they are not privy to the basic facts. At the judgment, the consequence of our choices will be set and nothing can be changed beyond our resurrection. *Luke 16* Simple sounding choice, but not a choice easily made by most of the world. The majority of the world population knows nothing of this vital choice.

Remember when you became aware of heaven and hell.

_____

_____

_____

_____

More than sixty percent of the world population are completely unaware of the truth by Jesus Christ. Others have the information but ignore it. *Matt 11:27 All things have been delivered to Me by My Father, and no one knows the Son except the Father. Nor does anyone know the Father except the Son, and the one to whom the Son wills to reveal Him. NKJV*

Since sin entered the world, every man puts a barrier between himself and God. To be with God again we must know the way to remove the sin barrier and reconnect with God. **The gospel is the good news of God's Son who can take away the barrier and bring us back in the family of God.** From the time of Adam and Eve, all people of the whole world have needed a Savior, and God promised one because He never stopped loving the creation made in His own image. The first prophecy of salvation came just prior to God's pronouncement of the first punishment of expelling Adam and Eve from the garden of Eden when he promised to bruise the head of Satan *Gen. 3*. Thus began a cycle of God's blessings flowing to those who obeyed and punishment to those who disobeyed. His selection of Abraham's family to be the chosen family came about because of Abraham's willingness to obey when God sent him on an unknown journey and promised that through his lineage the whole world would be blessed *Gen. 12*. Abraham and Sarah believed Him. *Heb. 11:8-11*

Old Testament Precedent
Please read these verses and jot down a key phrase you find relevant and discuss.

Jer. 23:5 _____

Isa. 7:14 _____

Mic. 5:2 _____

Ps.118:22_____

Isa. 53:6_____

Ps. 72:17_____

"You're not the boss!" is the phrase used frequently by many children and some spoiled adults. Most of us willingly submit to the authority of a boss who pays well, especially if the work assigned is pleasant and meaningful. That is exactly what we have in the church: pleasant work with a great pay off! No, not a human boss: Jesus Christ is Lord. All authority has been given to Him by the Father. *Matt. 28:18 And Jesus came and spoke to them, saying, "All authority has been given to Me in heaven and on earth. Go therefore and make disciples of all the nations, baptizing them in the name of the Father and of the Son and of the Holy Spirit," NKJV* He's the boss and we are slaves to Him. He bought us at a great price and the reward He offers for our submission and adoration is eternal bliss.

Since the Bible is a large book with many commands, how do we know what we are to do? How we are to think and behave? By going to the Authority. *John 12:49 For I have not spoken on My own authority; but the Father who sent Me gave Me a command, what I should say and what I should speak. 50 And I know that His command is everlasting life. Therefore, whatever I speak, just as the Father has told Me, so I speak." NKJV* Jesus, in turn, passed authority to the apostles to teach the gospel just as He had received it from the Father. Paul wrote in *1 Cor. 9:18 That when I preach the gospel, I may present the gospel of Christ without charge, that I may not abuse my*
authority in the gospel. NKJV

What does the gospel mean to you personally?

_____

_____

_____

_____

_____

Jerusalem, on the day of Pentecost, was busier than a county fair; crowds of people greeting one another; aromas of meat and bread, animal dung, human sweat; shoulders jostling one another seeking passage to and from the temple. Jews, gathered in Jerusalem from several countries, speaking diverse languages, knew the prophecies of a Savior. Suddenly, voices were heard, speaking a language each understood, declaring that the Savior had been there, had been killed for their sins and had been seen alive after being buried, and was seen rising into the clouds to heaven. Was it true? Yes, three thousand believed! After asking what they should do, they were baptized into Christ. As days passed others obeyed in the same way and God added them to the church. Read this exciting report in *Acts 2*. We can even know exactly what Peter preached that day.

From Jerusalem, the gospel spread as Christians scattered to other parts of the world telling about the son of God in their new community. Preachers went forth working miracles to prove that the gospel they spoke was from God. Paul, after being blinded and shown Jesus in heaven, went to the people who are like most of us, non-Jews, declaring that Jesus died as sacrifice for the sins of ALL of US!! *1 John 2:1-2 And if anyone sins, we have an Advocate with the Father, Jesus Christ the righteous. 2 And He Himself is the propitiation for our sins, and not for ours only but also for the whole world. NKJV*

Describe how you felt when you knew you were lost and contrast it with how you felt after being baptized.

_____

_____

_____

_____

New Testament Admonition

Please read these verses and jot down a key phrase you find relevant and discuss.

Mark 1:1-2_____

Mark 16:15_____

Acts 14:21-23_____

Acts 15:7_____

Acts 20:24_____

Rom. 1:1-3_____

Rom. 1:16_____

Rom. 6:3-6_____

Rom. 10:15-16_____

Rom. 16:25_____

1 Cor. 4:15_____

Phil. 1:27_____

Phil. 4:3_____

Col. 1:23-24_____

1 Thess. 2:4_____

1 Peter 4:17-18_____

Rev. 14:6_____

1 Peter 1:25_____

2 Cor. 5:20-21_____

Because we know, we must tell others! We should be eager to tell the story of Jesus Christ who took our sins on Himself! How can we keep it a secret? Many are too timid to tell it for fear of being rejected by their friends. Jesus was rejected. Many do not feel qualified to teach someone. If you know what you did in order to obtain forgiveness, just tell of your own experience and reason for it. Many seem to think it is only for preachers to tell. Did Christ die only for preachers? If you can't speak it, then write it. If you can't write it, send a tract or a correspondence course. If you feel you can serve best in your own home or community, then teach there. If you are aware of lost people in far places, help send someone who wants to go. None of us should keep the gospel a secret because He said tell it. The songs, "Must I Go and Empty Handed" and "You Never Mentioned Him to Me" are great conscience prickers!

Jesus had His disciples go out with a partner when they were sent on the limited commission. Ask someone you respect to be your teaching partner or mentor. Just as with any new task, no one knows how to teach until they practice it. Probably the person you ask will be honored to have you as partner and will be uplifted by your request. After all, an experienced person was once a novice and needed help. No one is inspired in a miraculous way now, but we can definitely be inspired by the word and by the guidance of another dedicated Christian. Please do not think you are not good enough to teach the gospel.

After Paul became a Christian he spent the rest of his life telling others how to be saved even as he admitted terrible sin. *This is a faithful saying, and worthy of all acceptation, that Christ Jesus came into the world to save sinners; of whom I am chief.1 Tim 1:15 KJV* Forgiveness is an indescribably wonderful thing! Paul was able to convince many to turn from idolatry and deep moral sins to a life in Christ.

Make a list of people you hope will become Christians and begin to pray for them.

_____ _____

_____ _____

I, _____, will make sure that _____ knows how to become a Christian.

How will you do this?

_____

_____

Write It On Your Heart ♥ Memory verse: *Ps 55:16 As for me,*
I shall call upon God,
And the LORD will save me. NASU

Mama's granddaughter, Kerrie Flowers says, "Although not used much in our society these days, I purposefully choose to use the word 'obey' often. I have used it with our two daughters (age 14 and 13) their whole lives, and I use it daily when talking to my eighteen Pre K students. It is a word that carries WEIGHT.....much more so, in my opinion, than "mind" and "listen." Obey. As it rolls off the tongue, one senses that the word is above and beyond a mere earthly request....it is on a much larger and important spectrum! Our girls have asked us why we do/do not do certain things and while most times, we give them an honest answer with logical reasoning to it, sometimes we purposely tell them "because God tells us to (or not to)". We want them to know that while we won't always understand God's laws/rules, with FAITH and TRUST, we OBEY Him......... JUST BECAUSE HE SAID SO. And the same will be true sometimes when we tell the girls something..... our expectation is that they will/will not do it because they choose to

OBEY. We know God has our best interest at heart and He has called us to OBEY His Gospel. <u>SO WE DO.</u>"

Take It To Heart ♥ Fictional Dilemma for Obey the Gospel

I didn't use to worry like this. When Mother said I had been baptized as a baby I thought I was set, live today and go to heaven whenever. But Judy said a person who is baptized should believe and I didn't believe anything when I was only a baby. She said putting a bit of water on my head wasn't even baptism; that baptism is going under the water like the people in Acts did.

Judy may be right...but what will Mother say? I wish she would look in the Bible and see what it says but she thinks her priest has told her all she needs to know. No matter what Judy says, I will not do as she says! Lots of people are just like I am.

But the other night I saw Jamie baptized…I mean actually go under the water...it seemed exactly like what the man in Acts did...went down into the water. If Jesus comes tonight or tomorrow will He ask me why I didn't? Will I not go up to meet Jesus just because I haven't been under the water? I did a lot of wrong things but I haven't *killed* anybody… just told some lies, was rude to Eddie, well, that kind of thing… are they really sins? Will God hold it against me if just quit doing those things and start doing right all the time…Oh…I wish I could sleep. Judy said that Jesus told the apostles to go everywhere and tell everybody about Him and then baptize...she said Peter said repent and...for remission...maybe…

Write It From the Heart ♥ Memory of a person explaining the gospel

_____

_____

_____

_____

_____

_____

_____

_____

_____

_____

_____

_____

_____

_____

_____

_____

_____

_____

_____

_____

_____

_____

_____

_____

_____

_____

Mama's Cooking With Heart ♥
Blackberry Cobbler

Get up at dawn, apply kerosene to wrists, dress in a long-sleeved shirt and pants, and heavy shoes. Now perhaps the snakes and chiggers will not bite you. Climb the hill to the slope where blackberry bushes are hanging full of luscious wild blackberries.

Pick at least 5 gallons a day while the berries are plentiful.

Bring the berries home, disrobe, and take a bath. Sit down and breathe a minute.

Use dough left from making biscuits and add more lard. Roll it out on a floured space to a rectangle larger than the pan for the cobbler. Carefully lift it into the pan and press out the wrinkles. Wash the berries in cool well water and pick out any little sticks or leaves that may have fallen into the bucket. Take about 2 quarts of berries and add a couple of scoops of sugar with a little flour mixed in for thickening the juice that seeps out of the berries.

Fill the space inside the dough lined pan 2/3 full with the sweetened berries. Cover with another rectangle of thin dough. Sprinkle a good sized sprinkle of sugar on top and dot with little blobs of butter. Bake at 350 degrees for quite a while. Watch. When the top is brown and the juice is oozing out of little spaces it's done. Try to stay out of it until after dinner and give everyone else a fair chance.

Remember a "berry" nice experience with someone and record details.

MAMA SAID BE DIFFERENT

Family Heartstrums ♥

Aunt Mary opened her bag and gushed, "Louise, I've got the prettiest new shade of lipstick. Here, try this sample" as she handed a miniature tube to Mama. Anxiously I waited to see if Mama could spare any money from her Serbin factory check to order anything. Since Mama's red tube was still half full, I was elated when she relented and told Aunt Mary, "Ok, order that pink one," knowing it was for me. To make the deal even better, Aunt Mary always gave us two or three sample lipsticks and sprayed our wrist with some good-smelling cologne. When Mama put on a little make-up, wrapped her long brown hair up in an elegant French twist, there was no need for the short modern hairdos that her conscience would not allow her to have.

Sometimes, Mama was just plain different, from the world that is, in the important ways. She allowed us to be in style, with bobby socks, ponytails, circle skirts, but not in ways that interfered with Christian living. Even though she was well respected and loved by the community *as well as her church, her code of ethics was not manmade or based on a poll. It was odd that she, despite being well read on current events, would not vote in elections, because she believed, as David Lipscomb taught in his day, that the government was of the world.*

Heart of the Matter ♥

Ones who never tell a lie, say a curse word, wish harm for anyone, take an alcoholic drink, or make a sustained effort to avoid committing any of the sins listed in the Bible are really peculiar. The world beckons to us, tempting even the strongest to veer off the path led by Jesus. It is odd that many write letters or send correspondence courses to strangers with the hope that some will be receptive to the salvation offered by Christ. It seems odd that some will avoid the very appearance of evil by shunning gambling in any form or visiting places where "sin stays" unknown to those back home. Some different people choose not to encourage popularity won by compromise of Christian practices. Living by the standard set also by *Romans 14: 23 for whatever is not from faith is sin. NKJV*, makes use of the conscience, trained by daily Bible consultation, and demands some decisions to be different from the world and even different from some Christians. This standard of behavior can cause a bit of anxiety in our youth unless they are shored up by the adults in word and deed. A good philosophy is, "If you are not sure it's right with God, don't do it."

Remember a time when your parent would not allow you to do something others were doing. Record the event and your feelings. _____

_____

_____

_____

_____

_____

_____

Believing in the one God, Jehovah, is different from the majority of the world. Believers in Jesus Christ as God's Son make up an even smaller percentage of the world's population. Those who believe in His church as the exclusive saved body make up an even smaller percentage. A faith that requires a godly way of life involving worship and imitating Christ is held by a very small percentage of mankind. Many take the wide road but only a few take the narrow road that leads to life everlasting. *Matt 7:13-14.* In the book, **Let Us Go Again**, Betty Choate encourages women to partake in the divine nature of God by incorporating the attributes of Jesus that *seem* too lofty to apply (love your enemies, go the second mile, turn the other cheek, don't worry).

When Noah worked and preached, worked and preached, worked and preached for forty years to people who would not believe him; when he obeyed a God he could not see and had not made or could not touch; when he kept his family in control, he was different from every other person on earth. *Gen. 6* When he believed what God told him, he was different. When he even had a good thought, he was different, because the world at that time was evil continually. His sons must have taken some pretty tough ribbing for having a "crazy old man" for a dad. Can you imagine what the in-laws of Shem, Ham and Japheth must have thought about their daughters marrying into that odd man's family? How gratified the sons must have felt as the boat was floated up and over and the rain was still falling after 39 days! How proud they must have been that their dad had required them to swing a hammer and get aboard.

Weird boys were Daniel and his friends to prefer water over wine and beans over meat. Surely anyone would dive into food fit for the king himself! How vindicated they must have felt on judgment day when they were better looking and fleshier than the imbibers. *Dan. 1* Evidently God, the Father, truly knows what is best for the physical bodies he created. And that was only the beginning. Who would continue to pray to an invisible God knowing there were tattlers who wanted to make lion food of him? Who would continue to stand when the king had said bow down or be burned alive? Only those weird enough to believe and trust in God.

Remember a time when you or someone you know may have appeared weird for Christian behavior.

_____

_____

_____

Please read these verses and jot down a key phrase you find relevant and discuss.

Esther 3:8_____

Deut. 28:9-10_____

Lev. 11:45_____

Lev. 20:7-8_____

Deut. 7:6_____

Deut. 14:2_____

God selected the family of Abraham, Isaac, and Jacob as His people and gave them a law that taught them what sin was and what to do about it. As a result, the Israelites, when they were faithful, were very different from the other inhabitants of the world. In *Hebrews 11*, several people who lived their faith are recommended to us as examples of courageous, obedient people who believed in God and His promises. They worshipped a God *no one could see*; they killed the best of their animals and offered it to this God. They gave away a tenth of everything they earned. They didn't work at all or even walk very far on Saturday, the Sabbath. They did not cook a big midday Sabbath dinner and invite company. To the idolatrous world this must have seemed ridiculous! Unfortunately they often fell from this strange, righteous way and practiced the life style of their neighbors and enemies.

Being different is not in itself Godly. Being different may mean adapting one's own religion to include sin, such as assimilating the practice of polygamy, when the usual standard in the United States is monogamy. Some in our country like to dress in the Gothic fashion but a distinction aimed at being noticed is not a Godly practice. Praying long and piously in a public place was different from the practice of the ordinary Jews but Jesus condemned it and said the praise of men was their reward and earned no reward of God *Matt. 6:6*. Women are instructed by Paul to be modest, which means not calling undue attention to oneself. Christians are blessed by being different from the world, a called out group, peculiar as in belonging to God, and molded in the image of Jesus Christ.

New Testament Admonition

Please read these verses and jot down a key phrase you find relevant and discuss.

1 Peter1:15 _____

John 15:18-19 _____

John 17:14-17 _____

John 17:23 _____

Rom. 12:2 _____

1 Cor. 4:9-10 _____

James 1:27 _____

1 John 5:4-5 _____

2 Cor. 3:18 _____

Phil. 3:20-21 _____

1 Peter 2:9-12 _____

Jesus urged his followers to be the salt of the earth. He wants us to be humble when the world is advising that we should think highly of self. Getting even or paying back those who hurt us is actually useless because He explained that God would take care of retribution where it is deserved. Jesus advised us to seek the kingdom of heaven first rather than the riches of the world. The Sermon on the Mount lists behaviors and attitudes that seem unusual, such as mournful, meek, poor in spirit, etc. but a blessing is pronounced to those possessing those traits.

Can you imagine the astonishment of Philemon when he opened the letter from his good friend Paul and discovered that his slave was being sent back? He must have had a major adjustment in attitude to consider treating his slave as a brother. Shock is what he must have felt when he saw Onesimus strolling up the trail...coming back. Astonishment must have consumed Onesimus when Philemon treated him like a brother.

What an enormous amount of courage and trust it took for Onesimus to return to bondage! The power of the gospel will make us different from the ordinary world citizen.

Many years ago, Americans who traveled for short term mission work for Christ in the Caribbean were impressed at how well the young Christians of Trinidad had been taught. These youth spoke clearly of how their lives were different since they, "came out of the world" or how they had lived when they "were in the world". Also evident to those who watch, is the peculiarity of many Christian missionaries, exhibited by their willingness to go for extended periods far from loved ones, relinquishing many comforts Americans take for granted, and forsaking the financial gain of a secular profession.

Describe one change you made when you became a Christian.

_____

_____

_____

_____

Rom 8:16-17 The Spirit Himself bears witness with our spirit that we are children of God, 17 and if children, then heirs--heirs of God and joint heirs with Christ, if indeed we suffer with Him, that we may also be glorified together. NKJV

God has claimed us as His children! If anything can make us different from the world it is that we can call God our *Father.* He promised that we can inherit right along with His only begotten Son! We can be transformed from sinner to forgiven, from lost to saved, from servant of Satan to servant of God. Our mind can be transformed to think good thoughts, which will bring about good words and actions. *Eph 5:8 For you were once darkness, but now you are light in the Lord. Walk as children of light 9(for the fruit of the Spirit is in all goodness, righteousness, and truth), 10 finding out what is acceptable to the Lord. NKJV*

I,_____,will help_____
have the courage to live differently from the world and to appreciate the blessing of that difference.
How you will do this? _____

_____

_____

_____

Write It On Your Heart ♥ Memory verse: *Rom. 12:1 I beseech you therefore, brethren, by the mercies of God, that you present your bodies a living sacrifice, holy, acceptable to God, which is your reasonable service. NKJV*

Mama's granddaughter, KaRen Coffman says, "It is as important to stand up for God as it is to turn from evil."

Take It To Heart ♥ Fictional Dilemma for Christians Must Be Different
Jara and Ken had just moved to the outskirts of Shadow Vale and Sunday morning rolled around just on time. Big decision for today….what to wear? Bigger decision…what to let Ally wear? These California people are pretty casual but the "church people" may not be. Jara really hoped to fit in and be a part of this church family and first impressions are very important. Their web site showed they were involved in many good works and missions so

it seemed to be a potential church home.

If I wear a dressy suit, will they think I am too somber? If I wear casual slacks, will they think I am not respecting the Lord's day? I know Ally will want to wear those raggedy jeans but no way is she going into a new church group in those ratty things! Jara fumed.

Soon after breakfast, Ally came bouncing downstairs in, you guessed it, her favorite holey jeans and a top that barely covered her midriff when she was perfectly still. *Ok*, Jara, worried with lips clamped together. *New places are hard on teens, but if I let her go that way today, what about next week? I have never let her dress that way except at home....but here.... she has to fit in...and I want to fit in.....do we have to be odd ducks?* New place, new customs, new friends, what habits do we change?

_____

_____

_____

_____

Write It From the Heart ♥ Tell about a time when you felt conspicuous or left out.

_____

_____

_____

_____

_____

_____

_____

_____

_____

Mama's Cooking With Heart ♥
Banana Pudding

1 cup sugar	½ stick butter
1/3 cup flour	1 tbsp. vanilla
2 cups milk with cream	Box of vanilla wafers
3 eggs yolks separated from whites	4 or 5 bananas

Mix flour with sugar in a heavy saucepan. Slowly stir in milk. Turn on high heat for a few minutes and then down to medium. Beat yolks of eggs a little bit while liquid is heating. Dip about a half cup of warm mixture and mix into egg yolks. Pour it back into the saucepan stirring rapidly. Stand there, don't move away, stand there and keep stirring until the mixture becomes thick but not set. Take off the heat. Add the butter and vanilla and mix thoroughly.

To assemble:

Place a layer of vanilla wafers on the bottom of a casserole dish. Place a layer of banana slices over the wafers. Pour sauce over the two layers using enough to flow in all the spaces. Repeat once or until you run out of ingredients. Let the pleading youngster lick the pudding spoon. Optional: Use the egg whites to make meringue. Place on top of banana pudding and bake about 20 minutes at 350 degrees. Cool, serve, but save some for Dick who will be here in a little bit.

MAMA SAID FORGIVE AND ASK FOR FORGIVENESS

Family Heartstrums ♥

"You knew that floor was wet!" shrieked Bibbie as Jack leaped the fence into the hog lot to escape the broom she was swinging at empty air. Jack made himself scarce for a few hours knowing the house was not a safe place for him. Bibbie mopped up the mud he had tracked across the clean kitchen linoleum and allowed a Frank Sinatra croon from the WSM radio station to calm her frayed nerves. By the time Jack edged in to his place at the supper table set for eight, the experience was only a funny story.

I was terrified and furious when my brothers chased me with fishing worms and laughed at my misery but I quickly joined in when they needed another basketball player. It was impossible to stay angry with someone who taught me to swim in the creek, to catch and throw a softball, to play "cars" in the dirt, and to milk a cow before I realized milking was work.

*Every prayer at home contained the words,
"Please forgive us of our sins". If Mama needed to
be forgiven, surely everyone else does. Her words
were kind, her actions were good, she worshipped
regularly and studied the Bible to learn more
of God's will, yet she prayed for forgiveness. No,
they were not meaningless words.   One's thoughts
are private and who knows what sin of omission
might have troubled her.   She believed* Matt 6:14-
15 But if you do not forgive men their trespasses, neither will your
Father forgive your trespasses. NKJV *and taught that we
not only needed forgiveness but must also forgive
others. She had to forgive us kids plenty of times.*

Heart of the Matter ♥

Forgiveness is an ongoing part and natural part of childhood. Although children may not formally ask for forgiveness from one another, we were taught to ask God for forgiveness. Kids play, fight, get up and play again. Children find forgiveness an automatic response to ordinary misbehaviors when they have the opportunity to play after the offense. Parents, however, must intervene in bullying situations and direct the misbehaving child to repent and treat others respectfully.

A person who purposely hurts another is a person tormented with painful thoughts. If we keep that in mind, perhaps we will feel more empathy and have less desire to retaliate. Children may say, "I'll get you back if it is the last thing I do!" Usually the anger is soon forgotten without any serious retribution and they are friends again. Unfortunately, maturity changes our reactions. Adults may not lash out as quickly but many find forgiveness to be more difficult.

Remember an argument you had as a child and how quickly you resumed playing.

_____

_____

_____

_____

Joseph was a champion forgiver! After his brothers wanted to kill him but sold him into slavery instead, he knew better than to trust them. When they came to Egypt to buy grain and did not recognize this mighty 'Egyptian' as their brother, he put them through a few tests. He had money put into their sacks to see if they would be honest and return it; they did. He questioned them about their family in order to determine if they had treated his full brother, Benjamin, in the same shameful way they had treated him; they had not. Finally, after the ten brothers passed his tests, he identified himself as their brother and held no animosity toward them. With tears of joy he hugged them and welcomed them to Egypt. *Gen 50:19-21 Joseph said to them, "Do not be afraid, for am I in the place of God? 20 But as for you, you meant evil against me; but God meant it for good, in order to bring it about as it is this day, to save many people alive. 21 Now therefore, do not be afraid; I will provide for you and your little ones." And he comforted them and spoke kindly to them. NKJV*

David repeatedly tried to have an amicable relationship with King Saul even after Saul murderously pursued him. Twice, when Saul and his army searched for him, David came so near that he could have killed Saul, but he did not, choosing instead to respect God's anointed. After cutting off a piece of Saul's clothing as proof of his restraint, David called out to Saul from a distance and tried to reason with him, but Saul was beyond reasoning. King Saul seemed to comprehend that God was blessing David and obtained a promise from David not to annihilate his family from the face of the earth. *1 Sam. 24*

Remember a time when you were offended and tell how you managed to forgive. _____

_____

_____

_____

Old Testament Precedent

Please read these verses and jot down a key phrase you find relevant and discuss.

Ps. 25:18_____

Ps. 65:3_____

Ps. 79:9_____

Jer. 36:3_____

Ex. 34-6-7_____

Gen. 50:17-19_____

Peter approached our Lord and inquired, "How many times must we forgive someone?" He thought forgiving seven times was plenty. Jesus explained that, "Nope" seven is just getting started! Even seventy times seven is not the upper limit. *Matt.18: 21-22* He went on to speak the parable of the man who was forgiven a huge debt but in turn refused to forgive another man of a tiny debt and was severely punished for it.

Peter and the other apostles may have had difficulty forgiving Paul because of the harm he, as Saul, did persecuting their beloved Christian brothers and sisters in Jerusalem and round about. But being persuaded of Paul's sincere repentance and conversion, the apostles forgave him and included him into the close fellowship as a brother and an apostle to the Gentiles. They could readily see that God had forgiven him and was using him. Possibly Peter recalled with gratitude that God had forgiven him when he denied being a disciple of the Lord Jesus three times. Perhaps Thomas remembered when Jesus forgave him for doubting His resurrection. Perhaps Matthew remembered that God had forgiven him of his tax collector activities. How can we not extend forgiveness in view of our own need for forgiveness?

New Testament Admonition

Please read these verses and jot down a key phrase you find relevant and discuss.

Matt. 6:12-15_____

Matt. 9:6_____

Luke 17:3_____

Luke 23:34_____

1 John 1:9_____

Acts 5:31_____

Acts 13:38-39_____

Acts 26:17-18_____

Eph. 1:7-8_____

Acts 8:22_____

2 Tim. 4:14-15_____

Rom. 12:17-18_____

Victims of crime feel they did not deserve such treatment. A spouse deceived by an adulterous partner feels betrayed. A parent whose child is harmed may feel their own heart is stabbed. A person maligned by a brother or sister in Christ may suffer anguish.

We may want to retaliate but Jesus did not, knowing that those who refuse to repent and seek forgiveness will suffer in due time. When James and John suggested bringing down fire from heaven to devour a village of Samaria, Jesus rebuked them. *Luke 9:52-55.*

Lives have been ruined by a person's own inability to forgive. "Getting even" is a foolish, useless behavior. *Heb 10:30 For we know Him who said, "Vengeance is Mine; I will repay," says the Lord. And again, "The LORD will judge His people." NKJV* Our attempts to get even would be insignificant compared to what God will do. *2 Thess. 1:6* states, *"...it is a righteous thing with God to repay with tribulation those who trouble you," NKJV* Harboring grudges causes physical and mental ill health and sweeps away happiness. The spirit of God brings us peace, not nightmares; He brings us joy, not ill will toward others, He brings us hope, not dread. How shocked the listeners must have been when Jesus said, *But I say to you, love your enemies, bless those who curse you, do good to those who hate you, and pray for those who spitefully use you and persecute you. Matt. 5:44 NKJV*

But how? How can one forgive someone who has wreaked havoc with their life? The only way to forgive others is to remember that Jesus left heaven to come to earth and suffer as we do. He was beaten with stripes and spat upon. After healing the sick and infirm He was called names and accused of being from Satan. *Matt. 12: 24 But when the Pharisees heard it, they said, "This man does not cast out demons except by Beelzebul, the ruler of the demons." NKJV* He was betrayed by one chosen to be one of the apostles who traveled with him, ate with him, heard him teach, and witnessed the miracles. His cousin, John, who prepared the way for Him, was beheaded. His own earthly brothers were reluctant to believe he was actually God's son. John 7:5 *For even His brothers did not believe in Him.* NKJV Then we must each remember, it was **my sin** that put Jesus on the cross, **my sin** that caused God to turn away, and **my sin** that required Him as a perfect sacrifice.

When the adulterous woman was brought before Jesus, the accusers were surprised that He chose to forgive her when she deserved to be stoned, according to the law of Moses. *Leviticus 20:10* Rather than submit to their sly pressure, Jesus invited any perfect man to throw the first stone. When none dared toss a single rock, Jesus dismissed her with these words, *"Then neither do I condemn you, ...Go now and leave your life of sin." John 8:11 NKJV* When we ask God to forgive us we must also be determined to correct the fault and not continue in sin.

Two kinds of sin must be dealt with: 1) those overt things we think, speak, or do that are wrong and 2) those good things we fail to do. *James 4:17* More often we concentrate on avoiding overt sin, but just imagine how wonderful the world would be if we all did all the things we know to be right. Think of all the kind deeds, all the mercy, all the good teaching that would transform our community. Sounds like heaven, doesn't it?

Remember a time when you were tempted to get even with an offender. _____

_____

_____

_____

_____

_____

Jesus told His disciples that unless we become like little children we cannot enter the kingdom of heaven and took the children and blessed them. Could it mean that we should be like children who are quick to forgive a playmate? Could it mean that we should be like children with an absolute faith without having to understand all the *hows and whys*? **Remember a time when someone dear to you forgave you of an offense.**

_____

_____

_____

Our youngsters also must forgive their parents, teachers, and grand-parents for mistakes. Just ask almost any teenager and you will find out that the adults in authority over them are not without fault. Adults should model extending forgiveness and asking for forgiveness when a mistake is made.

Write It On Your Heart ♥ Memory verse: *Ps 86:5 For You, Lord, are good, and ready to forgive, And abundant in loving kindness to all who call upon You. NASU*

Commitment: I, _____, will endeavor to train _____ to forgive others as he/she wants to be forgiven.

Mama's granddaughter, Kelly Buchanan says, "I need to be forgiving because according to the scripture if I am NOT then He won't forgive me."

Take It To Heart   ♥   Fictional Dilemma for Forgive

Shovesta knew she could never get over what had happened, not ever. She could overlook his forgetting her birthday or anniversary, but not this, not ever! Not only was her husband unfaithful, but it was with *her,* the traitor who pretended to be a trustworthy friend. Two years ago when they entered the financial advisor's office, Shovesta knew she needed advice on how to manage the windfall she had received when her grandmother died. It was so much more than she expected that her mind stalled when she tried to decide where to save it or where to invest it or what on earth to do with it. James had urged her to go see Amee and to take her advice as she was a financial whiz, experienced in handling large amounts of money belonging to her clients.

Experienced all right, experienced in stealing husbands, in funneling money to off shore accounts, and experienced in breaking hearts. The Lord says to forgive, so that we may be forgiven. The Lord said turn the other cheek. The Lord says He will repay, but Shovesta wondered if she would ever see that day. They deserved to be punished, but *she* was the one being punished. How will she ever forgive and have peace again when she has lost her husband and most of her grandmother's fortune? How will she ever get past the anger at such a betrayal?

Write It From the Heart ♥ Memory of Childhood Forgiveness

_____

_____

_____

_____

_____

_____

_____

_____

_____

_____

_____

_____

Mama's Cooking With Heart ♥

Ham and Red Eye Gravy.

Go out into the cold smokehouse and find the cured ham hanging from the rafters. Use a sharp butcher knife to cut out a large chunk. Back in the kitchen; slice the ham into at least eight thin slabs, one for each family member. Heat the black iron skillet and lay in the ham slices flat. Turn the heat down and let the ham fry until the fat edges become clear, indicating doneness. Turn the ham slices and cook the other side. Watch and see that the ham does not burn. The skillet will not hold all the slices so cook in batches, 3 or 4 slices at the time according to how much area the slabs cover. Remove from the skillet and place on a large platter. Don't salt....Daddy did that when he cured them.

Pour about a cup and a half of water in the skillet where the ham was cooked and the rendered brown fat, grease, remains. Watch it sizzle and scrape up the bits from the bottom. Pour into a gravy bowl. That's red eye gravy. Anyone who loves it will spoon it over an open biscuit. (Some mothers used coffee instead of water.)

Ham may be served with eggs, scrambled or fried. Or just place inside a biscuit. Um Um Good!

MAMA SAID GO TO CHURCH

Family Heartstrums♥

"Come on, Mark," were the only words required from Daddy to get one of the boys perched in front of him and the clip, clip, clip of scissors and buzzzz of clippers began. "Be still, Tommy. I don't want to gap your hair." Daddy snipped my brothers' Sunday morning haircuts every two weeks and any kid old enough was urged to apply Griffins shoe polish on their slippers or spread Vaseline on our black patent leather Sunday shoes. As a tenant farmer's wife before Daddy was able to buy his own farm, Mama coped with laundry using water pumped from a well and heated in an outdoor kettle over an open fire. She doused the youngsters in a No. 2 washtub, and spent hours ironing starched shirts and dresses. Getting a large family spic and span for Sunday school and worship every week was a tremendous task.

One Sunday morning when the snow was too deep for most folks to venture out of Gingerbread Holler, we piled into the car and Daddy drove *us up and over the hills, over unplowed, rough, gravel roads made smooth and slippery to worship services. Mama just did not miss worship services, so when she asked, "Ben, can we make it?" he made sure we did. We could have worshipped at home but what an impression this effort made on our youthful minds.*

When her children grew up, began dating, driving, and becoming independent, Mama's words were, "If you are going anywhere, you should go to church." This advice has continued to be one of the standards of Christian living for her descendants these decades after her death. During our teenage years when we were permitted to attend any neighboring congregations of the Lord's body on Sunday night, we sometimes went to the "town" congregation with a date, but the strong advice from Mama was to worship somewhere.

Heart of the Matter ♥

Even today, with plenty of conveniences for getting a family ready to attend worship, preparation is still necessary. Children still need clean underwear even though it might still be in the dryer. The most essential element is the firm decision that the family will attend every Sunday. If one of the parents is not a Christian, this decision is more difficult and may come with a price, but it must be made without any wavering. Refusing to allow a young athlete to participate in a sport event that interferes with worship or Bible study is difficult. Someone must see that the family has enough sleep by getting in bed on Saturday night at the hour that allows adequate rest. A sleepy child is a grouchy child when he is pulled from a warm blanket and attempting to drag out a wilted teenager is next to impossible.

Hopefully, some Bible school teachers expect the Bible lesson to be studied before class as any child will learn more if he has studied a lesson and then hears it discussed in class. Just as with a school day, a brain fueled by breakfast thinks and learns better. Many of these loving tasks are carried out by the mother, but an involved father who leads the family will pitch in with decision making and the physical work.

Tell some funny or odd thing that happened one Sunday morning as you were preparing to attend church services either as a child or an adult.

_____

_____

_____

_____

Why should we worship? From the very first family, the inhabitants of earth were taught to worship God. As our Creator, He has the right to be worshipped and to be honored in the way that He chooses to be worshipped. From the record in Genesis, we know that when God completed each day's work, he declared that it was good. He did AWESOME work!! The scope of creation from the infinity of space to the minute world of microscopic life and the evidence of the interdependence throughout is actually more than my human mind can fully grasp. How He could even imagine such an existence, much less bring it into being, is beyond human comprehension. How He now brings little baby boys and girls to our families and establishes such love is an indescribable, inexplicable gift.

So can His promise of a created heaven be understood? Even though the symbols used in Revelation give us a mental image, our human minds may not clearly understand the perfection of heaven. Nevertheless, we *can believe* it because His earthly creation, which *is* visible, shouts of His handiwork. The immeasurable love we feel for our own families gives us an inkling of God's love.

Think of a time you were tempted to miss worship services and tell how you resisted the temptation. _____

_____

_____

_____

We know from the Genesis account of Cain and Abel that He does not accept just anything some claim as worship, but He appreciates those who truly honor him. Cain worshipped partially when he offered a sacrifice, but it was not what God wanted and He was displeased. Just as we love to receive gifts that reflect that someone knows our preferences and just as we are displeased with gifts that show someone has totally ignored our taste, so God is. He has told us how he prefers to be worshipped. In spite of God's specific instructions on how He wished to be worshipped, some chose to do it their own way. If we love Him, we will keep His commandments. It is written that we may know that God approved the worship of Abel and disapproved the worship of Cain who did it his own way.

Ignorance is not an excuse as exposed in the example of Uzzah who touched the precious ark of the covenant against God's specific command of keeping it holy, away from contamination of human touch (2 Sam. 6:1-8). Offering strange fire in worship was not accepted as we see in the case of Nadab and Abihu (Leviticus 10). In a faint comparison, would you feel loved if a relative knew that you despised orange yet gave you an orange coat for your birthday?

Old Testament Precedent
Please read these verses and jot down a key phrase you find relevant and discuss.

Deut. 26:10_____

2 Kings 17:36_____

Ps. 29:2_____

Zeph. 2:11_____

Zech. 14:16-17_____

Relate one incident recalled from your childhood worship services.

_____

_____

_____

Jesus, Himself, quoted scripture, proving to Satan that He would only worship God, that He wanted to please His Father. *Matt 4:10* Then Jesus said to him, *"Away with you, Satan! For it is written, 'You shall worship the LORD your God, and Him only you shall serve." NKJV*

Jesus worshipped God in the temple, beginning when He went there as a twelve year old. His knowledge and depth of understanding amazed the teachers in the temple those three days. He taught the woman at the well that God wants us to worship Him in the right way wherever we are. *"God is Spirit, and those who worship Him must worship in spirit and truth." John 4:24* NKJV Jesus needed to communicate with His Father in prayer and went to be alone in order to do so.   He prayed before He was tempted by Satan; He prayed when He was transfigured; He prayed for the little children; He prayed before He ate; He prayed before He was captured and crucified. Using what we call 'the Lord's prayer', He modeled the correct way to pray and taught His disciples to pray. Warning us that some worship does not please Him, Jesus said, *"And in vain they worship Me, Teaching as doctrines the commandments of men."* *Matt 15:9 NKJV*

Worshipping was extremely important to the first Christians who met and worshipped daily, *Acts 2.*   *James 2:2* speaks of the assembly and we know that some of them were lengthy. *Acts 20:7 Now on the first day of the week, when the disciples came together to break bread, Paul, ready to depart the next day, spoke to them and continued his message until midnight.* NKJV

Following the pattern set by inspired apostles and the early Christians, we know we should worship on Sunday as they did. Taking the Lord's supper on the first day of the week as Jesus asked us to do is essential to keep us aware of the sacrifice that could have been made by no other. What a small thing to ask us to do when we compare it to what He did for us! To neglect such a ritual is to proclaim His death as insignificant.

New Testament Admonition

Please read these verses and jot down a key phrase you find relevant and discuss.

1 Cor. 11: 20-26_____

John 4:23-24_____

Acts 17:23-25_____

Heb. 1:6_____

Heb. 2:12_____

Phil. 3:3_____

1 Cor. 14:15_____

Col. 3:16_____

Eph. 5:19_____

James 5:13_____

Remember a time when you or someone you know had trouble keeping a young child quiet during the worship service and tell how the problem was solved.

_____

_____

_____

_____

Remember a blessing you received when you visited a worship service at another congregation than your home congregation. _____

_____

_____

_____

Humanity has a need to worship. If the real true God is not known, then a false one will be worshipped. The Bible tells of the creator, the I Am, the Alpha and the Omega, Jehovah. We are told that the only way to the Father is through the Son, Jesus Christ. *John 14:6 Jesus said to him, "I am the way, and the truth, and the life; no one comes to the Father but through Me. NASU*

Following God's command and the example of inspired apostles leads us to worship in a manner that pleases God. How dare we substitute our own way when He revealed how we should worship? He wants us to pray as Jesus taught the apostles and early Christians did. He wants us to sing; the apostles and Christians of the New Testament did. Jesus told us to remember Him and his sacrifice by eating unleavened bread and drinking fruit of the vine; the apostles and early Christians did. The inspired writer, Paul, told us to study and learn through hearing his Word; the apostles and early Christians did. God wants us to live holy lives showing awe of our Savior. *Rm. 12:1, 2*

Singing helps us feel the awesomeness of our Father as our emotions are tapped by the words of a praise song or an homage to the sacrifice Jesus made. Some songs lead us in collective prayer and others are powerful motivators for the sinner to obey. Truth spoken in songs is a method of teaching and verses set to music are easily learned. If we pay attention to the words our heart strings will strum and Jehovah will accept our worship.

Commitment: I, _____, will make worship of God through Jesus Christ a priority in my life and will use my influence to help train _____ to follow the same Godly practice.

How will you do this?_____

_____

_____

_____

Memory verse: *Rev 15:4 Who shall not fear You, O Lord, and glorify Your name?   For You alone are holy. For all nations shall come and worship before You, For Your judgments have been manifested." NKJV*

♥ **Mama's granddaughter, Kerrie Flowers says**, "Go to church" ….there is so much *good* and *truth* in that wise instruction, yet so much "incompleteness". I have learned that "going to church" is not so much the goal, but the *natural result/effect* of a heart that is in tune with God's will for his/her life. If we have a genuine desire to follow Jesus, "going to church" happens naturally after we put Him on through baptism. There is no thought of "should we go today?" or "man, I could really use this time to (you fill in the blank)". That thought process is nailed to the cross and in its place is a deep *yearning* to be with our brothers and sisters in Christ...communing, singing, praying, and bearing one another's burdens joyfully. Life is short....if one is not in a place where that is happening with his/her church family, then find somewhere where it can happen. We drive 45 minutes to church now and it has been the best decision we have made as a family!! *Joyful and sincere worship* gets us through the week like nothing else can. So yes, "Go to church." But first, *commit your whole being to Jesus....* He will lead you to His body through the study of His Word.

Take It To Heart ♥ Fictional Dilemma for Worship

Nothing is going my way. I've gained so much weight that nothing looks good on me. Those people don't care if I come or not. They don't even speak…well, I actually didn't want them to and I got out of there as quick as possible. It's not like the church where I used to go. Everyone here is so well dressed and their hair and nails are perfect and I look a mess. I couldn't sleep last night and my eyes are puffy.

Not just that, but does it do any good? The argument with Thomas last night was wrong…I knew it but it still happened. Why go to worship if I'm going to come home and do wrong again? He wants us to take the day and do something fun….maybe he's right….maybe we should just go somewhere, anywhere, to get our minds off our worries. After all we worked hard all week, even overtime....surely we deserve one day to do as we please.....but I want to please God....will I be happy if I do as I please and it doesn't include God?

Write It From the Heart ♥ Memory of a song that struck a chord in your heart

_____

_____

_____

_____

_____

_____

_____

_____

_____

_____

_____

_____

_____

_____

_____

_____

_____

_____

_____

_____

_____

Mama's Cooking With Heart ♥
Tea Cakes

2 eggs   1 ½ cups sugar   ½ cup lard   4 cups self-rising flour
1 tsp. vanilla   Preheat oven to 400 degrees F.

Mix lard and sugar well. Add eggs and vanilla. Add flour to shortening mixture until dough is stiff and doesn't seem sticky (you may not need to add all of the flour). If you put too much add a little milk.

Roll out on a floured board. Cut into circles with a cookie cutter or a glass rim dipped in flour. Re-roll trimmings and cut into circles until all of the dough has been used. Bake on lightly greased cookie sheets for 8 to 9 minutes.

Boiled Chocolate Icing

In a heavy saucepan, combine a cup of sugar with 2 tablespoons or so of cocoa. Add a half cup of milk, or cream if you want it to be really good. Bring it to a full boil for about a minute. Don't leave it or it will surely burn! Take it off the heat and add a small chunk of butter and a teaspoon of vanilla. Tilt the pan until it puddles at the lower edge and beat it a little bit with a big spoon. *Beat* means to stir vigorously bringing the spoon up for air. When tea cakes are cool, cover each one with chocolate icing. Leave on the kitchen table to wait for kids to get off the school bus.

Dear Reader,

Please use any blank pages or spaces for your own creative voice by writing stories, memories, poems, prayers or making doodles or drawings. I hope this book has been a happy experience from my heart to yours, knowing that your memories are treasures that deserve preservation!

Maxie

m.fortner@mchsi.com

"♫I owe a debt I cannot pay " Adapted lyrics by Ellis J. Crum

Song title: It Won't Be Very Long ♫ by Morgan Williams and E.M. Bartlett

Song title: I Believe In the One They Call Jesus ♫
by Alton H. Howard

Song lyrics: ♫ What Will Christ Do With Me? by Vana R. Raye H. R. Russell copyright 1948
by L. O. Sanderson

Made in the USA
Middletown, DE
23 November 2021

52791138R00096